GREAT AIRCRAFT AND THEIR PILOTS

Great Aircraft and their Pilots

Roy Cross

HUGH EVELYN   LONDON

First published in 1971 by Hugh Evelyn Ltd.,
9 Fitzroy Square, London W1P 5AH.
© 1971, Roy Cross.
Typeset by Specialised Offset Services Limited, and
Printed in Great Britain by A. Wheaton & Company.
Designed by E.W. Fenton.
S.B.N. 238.78976.4

Contents

Preface

NO LESS THAN the great sagas of exploration by land and sea which punctuate recorded history, the early pioneering flights and trailblazing intercontinental aerial voyages—more recent in time but of equal portent—appeal to those with a sense of history and an admiration for the adventurous and the courageous. The epic air battles of the past forty-odd years likewise hold the same fascination for many as the classic military campaigns and naval engagements which have moulded the course of civilisation. Modern air power has changed history in the same way as the exercise of sea power and the movements of great armies; indeed it has become for a time and in conjunction with the intercontinental nuclear missile the ultimate weapon and arbiter of man's fate.

Aviation history is overflowing, too, with great personalities; the exploration of the air and the use of it as a fighting arena demanded the same courage and tenacity that spurred on the great soldiers, sailors and explorers of the past, and exacted a like toll in lives lost. Few of man's mechanical contrivances hold more technical interest than the aeroplane and involve so many facets of engineering technology as well as pure science. The atmosphere is an element completely foreign to man, and his mastery of the air is the greatest of his purely physical achievements save only for the conquest of space itself.

All these aspects of our aeronautical heritage are touched upon in this book. The dominant theme is the changing shape and technical development of the aeroplane in the span of thirty-eight years between two vital aviation landmarks: the first crossing of the English Channel by aeroplane in 1909, which as well as being a remarkable feat of personal courage and technical achievement simultaneously revealed the aeroplane as an entirely new potential vehicle of transportation and a possibly deadly military threat; and the breaking of the 'sound barrier' in 1947 which opened the way to modern aeronautical technology highlighted, for example, by the Concorde supersonic airliner.

These machines were no mere lifeless lumps of wood, canvas and metal. The human hand on the controls galvanised them into throbbing life, guided them to the four quarters of the earth or transformed them into deadly weapons. The deeds and personalities of their famous pilots are touched upon in the essays accompanying the main illustrations.

The twenty-one general arrangement drawings of aircraft were prepared with a dual purpose in mind. They combine the qualities of a conventional engineering drawing with the exterior form, detail and finish associated with the photograph. Thus they have, it is hoped, some visual appeal as a realistic impression of each historic aeroplane from several aspects while at the same time providing the essential working plans which would enable the legion of aircraft modellers to construct an accurate replica, to which end several cross-sections are provided as a guide to the precise form of wings and fuselage.

In order to reproduce the drawings as large and as clearly as possible the plan view is a dual-aspect representation, showing the top of one half of the plane adjacent to the bottom view of the same half (just as though the half plane had rolled over on its back). A disadvantage of this method is that one half of the aeroplane is not shown in plan view and any assymetric details and markings thereon must be ascertained from the front elevation or the accompanying text and photographs. Notes on the external colourings and markings are usually given in the text.

Although additions, corrections and many new photographs have been incorporated, the bulk of this material was published originally some years ago as a series of articles in a United States periodical. Given the general theme of great aeroplanes and their pilots, the choice of subject was left to the author and the collection is not intended as an assessment of the twenty-one most famous aeroplanes (though many of them would certainly feature in such a selection) but a cross-section including not only the universally-known personalities like Bleriot and Lindbergh and planes such as the Spitfire and Messerschmitt Bf 109, but many subjects less familiar to the general public that nevertheless made important contributions to aeronautical progress.

Nor is there any special significance in the nationalities involved; although those countries most advanced in the technological sense preponderate in this book, there can be few minor and none of the major powers except perhaps China which did not contribute their full share to the evolution of the aeroplane as a transport vehicle and as a weapon.

Sources of information and individual credits were itemised in the original articles and are summarised below. Special acknowledgement is made to William Winter and Walt Schroder, successive editors of *Model Airplane News,* New York, for their help and encouragement during the preparation of the original series, and to the following institutions, companies and individuals who contributed research material and photographs:— the Royal Aeronautical Society; National Aeronautical Collection, Science Museum; Imperial War Museum; Hawker Siddeley Group Ltd; Vickers Ltd; Fokker;*American Aviation Historical Journal; Flight;* United States Air Force; Smithsonian Institution, Washington, DC; *National Geographic Magazine*; Republic Aviation Division, Fairchild Hiller Corporation; Bell Aerospace Corporation; Bruce Robertson, Jack Bruce, Phillip Jarrett, J.D. 'Doug' Carrick, Ken McDonough, André Pernet, Roger A. Freeman and Jean Noel.

Bleriot's cross-channel aeroplane

AT 4.51 A.M. ON SUNDAY MORNING, 25 July 1909, Louis Bleriot took off from the dunes at Les Baraques village near Calais on his hazardous attempt to fly the English Channel. Only recently on 13 July he had won the Prix de Voyage of £560 offered by the Aero Club de France for the first cross-country aeroplane flight of 25 miles lasting not more than six hours–his time was actually 56 min 10 sec. Now he was competing for a £1000 prize offered by Lord Northcliffe and the *Daily Mail* for the first cross-Channel flight by an aeroplane.

Another Frenchman, Hubert Latham, had already attempted the crossing on 19 July in his graceful Antoinette, only to end up ingloriously in the Channel when his motor cut out at 1000 ft on a windless but misty morning. Latham even now was ready with a new machine to start on a second attempt. He was awakened that morning just in time to learn that Bleriot was already away. Feverishly he rushed away to get out his machine but the wind was now too strong to attempt a flight. Two days later he again took off from the French coast and got within a mile of the Dover foreshore before his engine again failed and he came down in the sea.

Still a third contestant, the Comte de Lambert, was planning to start from near Boulogne in a Wright machine which, however, he wrecked on a trial flight.

The little Bleriot monoplane had been rolled over from its makeshift shelter on the low sandhills at an early hour and Bleriot, who had been about since 2.30 a.m., had already taken it aloft to test the engine and controls and gauge the weather. The wind was reckoned to be rising but Bleriot, after a brief consultation with his companions, restarted the motor and took off, heading out over the channel to disappear gradually into the haze. Just before he started he had inquired almost as an afterthought, 'Tell me, where is Dover?' and the vague direction had been pointed out to him by his friend Leblanc, 'C'est là-bas.'

Now he was out over the Channel, soon out of sight of the French coast and of the escorting destroyer *Escopette* and with no indication of just where lay the mist-shrouded English shore. The

Slightly shaken after his heavy landing in the North Fall Meadow, Bleriot is helped along, followed by the French tricolour.

Monsieur and Madame Bleriot standing by a Bleriot XI with wings folded for transportation.

machine was badly underpowered, the temperamental three-cylinder Anzani engine giving a questionable output varying between 22 and 25 hp. Every foot of height had to be fought for, every turn would lose him some of the valuable height so laboriously gained, and he could not get above 300 feet. At the mercy of any sudden gust which blew down the Channel, his success depended upon the unpredictable performance of the clattering Anzani, which before had overheated after a bare twenty minutes running.

All that could be seen as he looked around was a mist-shrouded horizon and the grey oily waters below, and he must have had the beginning of that panic which creeps over a man stumbling about in a strange pitch-black room, groping and blind. True to form the motor began to overheat and lose power and the sea beneath loomed closer. It looked as though the second great Channel attempt would also have a watery end.

Just as things were looking desperate the machine ran through a rain squall which cooled the overheated cylinders. The motor again settled down to a steady clatter and presently Bleriot caught sight of the English cliffs through the haze.

Out in mid-Channel away from sight of land he had unconsciously veered eastwards with the wind and now found himself nearer Deal, miles northeast of Dover. Still well over the sea he swung south parallel to the coast looking for the castle and harbour of Dover and the spot where a journalist acquaintance, M. Fontaine of *Le Matin,* was waiting with a large tricolour flag to mark the landing place.

The light winds over the Channel had now freshened to 20-knot gusts, buffeting the tiny plane as it neared the coast. The landing approach was difficult and Bleriot finally put the machine down on the far-from-level North Fall Meadow almost under the walls of Dover Castle, damaging the landing gear and front end in the process. He was some way from the tricolour marker and for a moment, as he eased himself from the cockpit, was completely alone. The time was 5.28 a.m. The 31-mile flight had taken less than 40 epoch-making minutes, minutes which assured Bleriot and his machine an immortal place in the annals of great aerial endeavour, and made England, inviolable for centuries behind the Channel moat and an invincible navy, suddenly potentially as vulnerable as any Continental country to a new menace—from the air.

A British bobby puffing with the exertion was the first to arrive followed by Fontaine with his tricolour, and gradually a crowd gathered complete with a worried customs official with an armful of forms concerning contraband and infectious diseases. A stone memorial shaped roughly in the plan form of the machine is now embedded in the ground there, commemorating for all time one of the great moments in the history of aerial locomotion.

Aeroplane design in 1909 was largely a matter of guesswork and of copying features from machines which had already proved successful or at least able to take to the air. Against the current of contemporary opinion, which largely favoured the biplane, Bleriot had doggedly perfected his monoplane over

The scene shortly after Bleriot's heavy landing near Dover Castle on Sunday morning, 25 July 1909.

several years and many designs. The cross-Channel flight set the seal on the success of his design, and for several years to follow manufacturers and fliers all over the world copied or built under licence machines which made no attempt to disguise their Bleriot parentage.

In basic layout and in certain of its design details the Bleriot monoplane was far ahead of its time, setting the pattern for the fastest machines for decades ahead.

The two-bladed 6 ft 8 in diameter 10 lb propeller was made by Lucien Chauvière, the chief propeller manufacturer of the day. Although rated at 22-25 hp, the actual power of the air-cooled three-cylinder Anzani 'fan-shaped' engine during the flight was problematical. A very similar machine still maintained in airworthy condition in England and powered by an identical engine giving about 22 hp can scarcely gain height at all and there seems reason to guess that Bleriot boosted the power of the engine for some of his prize-winning flights. Bore and stroke were 105 by 130 mm, weight about 145 lb, and top revs around 1600 rpm. The compact unit was mounted in the nose by channel-steel brackets, the webs of which were perforated for lightness.

The fuselage was a wooden box girder, wire braced and covered in only at the sides in the vicinity of the cockpit. There was no top covering, nor flooring except a board mounting the rudder bar and control column. The wings were detachable to ease storage and transport and were built up around a main front spar, flexible rear spar, and other light intermediate spanwise members.

A model of the Bleriot XI.

Between the main aluminium-strip wood-reinforced ribs were wood stiffeners of about a quarter-inch section. The inside ribs and the spar ends of each wing were reinforced, the front spar being inserted in an aluminium box structure bridging the fuselage frame and the rear spar in special brackets in the cockpit sides, all bolted into place. The main spars were wire braced along the span to the front of a light tubular steel pylon atop and astride the front fuselage and to the main landing gear struts. Wing covering was Continental fabric.

The rear portion of the wing was flexible to give lateral control by warping, that is, by deflecting the trailing edge of one wing by hauling down on it with wire cables while simultaneously flexing the other wing rear edge upwards. In effect, the camber of one wing was increased, giving more lift that side, while the other was decreased with a loss

13

Above and right: *The Bleriot XI on exhibtion at the Paris Salon.*

of lift, thereby imparting a rolling motion to the machine. A subsidiary effect was that the wing with greater camber had increased drag which tended to slew the machine round. This had to be corrected with the rudder.

The Bleriot's warping wires ran from the control column via a pylon mounted beneath the cockpit to points on the rear spars, and the top equalising cables ran wing to wing across pulleys on the upper pylon. A patented universal-jointed control column was used, wing-warping and elevator-control wires being fastened to a bell-shaped fitting at the base of the vertical column, to which were also attached the two engine-control levers. The seat was a plain board, with a strap across the fuselage acting as a backrest, and there were no instruments.

The main and tail wheels employed an ingenious system of levered suspension similar in principal to that with which many modern aircraft are fitted. The main wheels were carried in a fork levered back from the bottom of the vertical landing gear strut, and braced by another fork extending upwards and forwards to a collar which slid up and down the column under impact and rebound. This movement was restrained by rubber cords in tension connecting the collar with the bottom of the vertical strut. The attachment points rotated about the column so that the main wheels could castor should the machine be drifting at touch-down in a cross-wind landing. A lot more was heard about cross-wind landing gear 30 years later in the 1940s. The castoring action on the Bleriot was damped and the wheels centralised in flight by bungee-sprung cross bracing wires between the

wheel forks. The tail wheel was similarly swivelled and centralised.

The tailplane was slung beneath the rear fuse-lage, attached to the bottom longerons by metal channel brackets. Outer sections rotated about the main tubular spar to act as elevators, and incidence could be altered by adjustment at a perforated metal strap securing the trailing edge and at two of the supporting struts.

A narrow fuel tank holding about three gallons was installed in front of the cockpit and next to it was a small oil reservoir pressurised from a hand-operated rubber bulb. Behind the pilot was a long cylindrical flexible air bag to give buoyancy in the event of a landing in the sea.

Few contemporary sources agree on the dimensions and other details of the cross-Channel Type XI. It was probably a one-off machine, specially prepared and differing in detail from the prototype first introduced in December 1908 at the Paris Salon, and from the production machines delivered in increasing quantities after the flight. It seems certain that the length was about 25 ft and the span 25 ft 6 in. Wing area was approximately 150 sq ft, chord well over six feet, and the gross weight, according to varying accounts, somewhere between 660 and 715 lb with fuel and pilot. It is generally accepted that the flight took 37 minutes at an average speed of about 48 mph.

Louis Bleriot was born on 1 July 1872 at Cambrai and trained at L'Ecole Centrale des Arts et Manufactures as an engineer. He made a comfortable fortune by inventing the Bleriot automobile headlamp and other electrical gear, which

14

gave him the wherewithal to experiment first with models and soon with full-size aircraft of widely varying types. Bleriot No 1 was an ornithopter of weird design which flew in model form but was a failure when translated into full scale. Bleriot blew up three engines, flapped the machine to pieces, spent a lot of money, and finally gave up aviation in disgust.

His interest was aroused again in 1905, and nearly all his income over the next few years went on a variety of designs which finally evolved into the Type XI. In all he made about £4000 from the Channel flight, started the first of several successful flying schools, and began to build airplanes in earnest. Between 1909 and 1914 he is said to have built 800 machines of 40 different types. After taking over the Deperdussin works in 1914, he was responsible for the production of the famous line of Spad aircraft, and when the First World War ended, his factory was producing 18 machines a day. After the war and until the firm was finally submerged in 1937 in the nationalisation of the French aircraft industry many famous aircraft of all types were produced.

On 27 July 1929 Louis Bleriot again crossed the Channel in a machine carrying his name to attend the Twentieth Anniversary Celebrations of his great flight. But this time he was a passenger in a big twin-engined Bleriot 127 multi-seat fighter of the French Air Force. He died seven years later in August 1936.

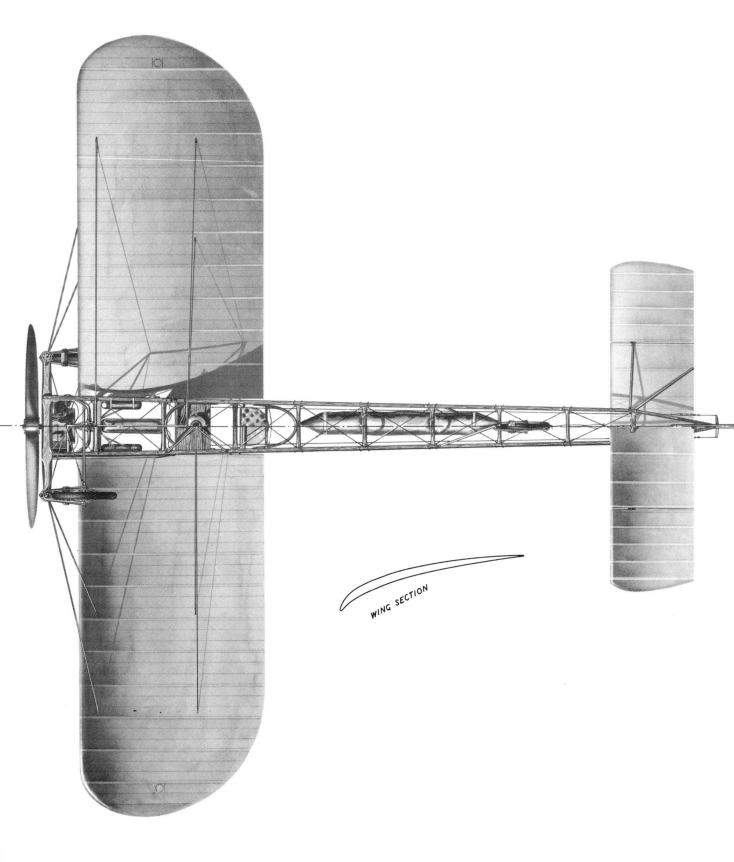

WING SECTION

0   5   8
FEET

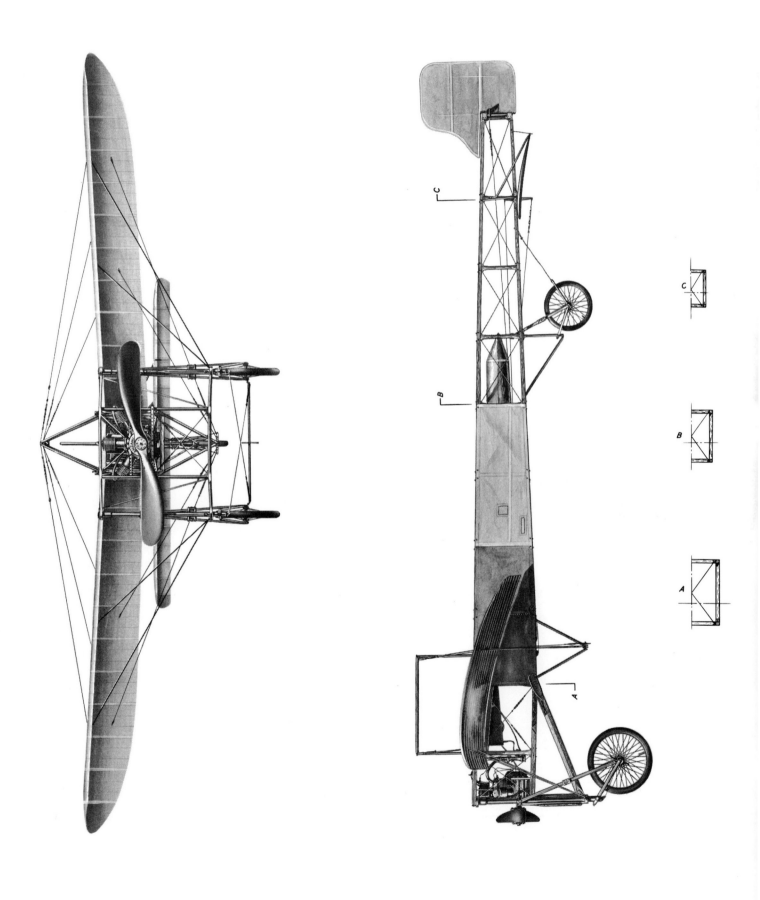

The Henri Farman Biplane

HENRI FARMAN was one of the chief participants in a great epoch of aviation history, the period 1908-1914, when the art of flying in Europe caught up with and finally overtook that fostered by the Wrights in the New World.

An Englishman who lived in France and became a naturalised Frenchman, Farman late in 1907 bought a machine from the famous Voisin brothers, who at that time were constructing for a number of aviators many of whom became famous in the next few years. Between then and 1908 Farman leaped into the limelight with a succession of flights which were unique in Europe though outclassed by the achievements of the Wrights (largely unknown or discounted in Europe until Wilbur's remarkable flying demonstrations in France beginning in August 1908).

At the end of 1908 Farman's machine was still very obviously of Voisin origin, with 'side curtains' between the four outer sets of interplane struts, but with embryo ailerons, 'balancing flaps', on all four wing trailing edge extremities. In May 1909 Farman flew a modified machine incorporating his own ideas, the main alterations being a greater gap between the wings and the elimination of the 'fuselage' of the Voisins in exchange for a simple chassis built on to the bottom wing to take the seat, fuel tank and engine, and strut extensions forward to support the single front elevator.

This machine, the monoplane Bleriot XI of cross-Channel fame and to a lessening extent the Wright, became the main inspiration of European constructors over the next year or two, being closely copied or built under licensing arrange-

Henri Farman at the controls of one of his biplanes.

An early Farman biplane, showing its clear derivation from the Voisin aeroplanes, at Issy les Moulineaux in July 1908.

ments in Britain as well as on the Continent, and to some extent in the USA where, however, the Wrights and Curtiss had a greater influence.

In 1910 Farman introduced the so-called 'Light Farman' of more compact dimensions, this machine becoming one of the main sporting and competition mounts in the ensuing years. Many variations of the basic design appeared, the drawing here representing a machine flown by Paulhan at the Lyons Aviation Meeting in May 1910 (and also the previous month when he won the £1000 *Daily Mail* prize for the first flight between London and Manchester).

The 1910 Farman had basically a two-bay wing layout, but some 'racing' machines, including Paulhan's, had the outer bay of the bottom wing removed, while Farman later added an extension bay on the top wing for some of his height and duration flights. One, two, or sometimes three rudders were fitted on individual machines.

Controls were operated from a universally-pivoted control column at the right of the seat and from a 'rudder bar' on the footrest extension. Forward movement of the 'stick' canted the nose of the front elevator down and, by means of connecting wires between front and rear elevators, forced the latter's trailing edge downwards. Pulling back the stick reversed the process. Sideways movement of the stick pulled down the balancing flap(s) on one side or the other, raising that wing. These hinged flaps hung loosely down when the machine was on the ground, and trailed horizontally in flight with the force of the airstream on them until pulled down on either side from the stick; they were not conventional double-acting ailerons as standardised later. The rudders had limited travel and were operated in a conventional manner from the footrest bar.

Aft of the pilot's position was a raised seat for a passenger, and behind this again a metal structure supporting the fuel and oil tanks. The 50-hp Gnome seven-cylinder rotary engine was the usual power unit, with the propeller mounted between it and the engine bearers. Wheels were mounted on strong skid structures and sprung with rubber cord. Dimensions varied according to the various modifications, but the 1910 machine usually spanned 34 ft 10 in and was about 38 ft long.

A close copy of the Henri Farman of this period was made by the British and Colonial Aeroplane

A Farman biplane at Hendon in 1911

Farman flying his biplane to win the distance record for a flight of 1500 meters in one minute twenty-eight seconds on 13 January 1908.

The Bristol Boxkite, British version of the Farman biplane.

Co. at Filton, Bristol, where today is assembled the British version of the BAC/Sud-Aviation Concorde supersonic airliner. So similar was the Bristol 1910 Biplane, or Boxkite, that Farman Brothers threatened to sue the English company, but the prosecution was dropped over the technicality of the Boxkite being 'improved' by Chief Engineer G.H. Challenger, and certainly the British machine was beautifully made with hand-picked timber and the finest materials.

Late in 1910 production was at the rate of two per week, at a selling price of £1100—of which £600 was accounted for by the French Gnome engine for which Bristols had secured the sole British agency. By the end of the year 16 machines had been built, and early the following year orders included eight for the Imperial Russian Army and four—later increased to eight—for the British War Office.

Customers for Farman's 1909 biplane numbered some 120, including the French and Russian Imperial Armies which took three and two machines respectively, while at least 34 individual clients ordered the 1910 model, Louis Paulhan

purchasing two, and the Russian Army bought an unspecified number.

These production figures from only one major and one secondary manufacturer give some indication of the interest in flying both as a sport and for military purposes only six or seven years after the very first aeroplane flight in 1903.

A replica of the Bristol Boxkite can be seen flying many weekends during the summer months at the Shuttleworth Collection flying demonstrations held at Old Warden Aerodrome near Biggleswade, Bedfordshire. Its lazy floating circuits of the tiny airfield revive the authentic flavour of those golden years of pioneer aviation before the First World War.

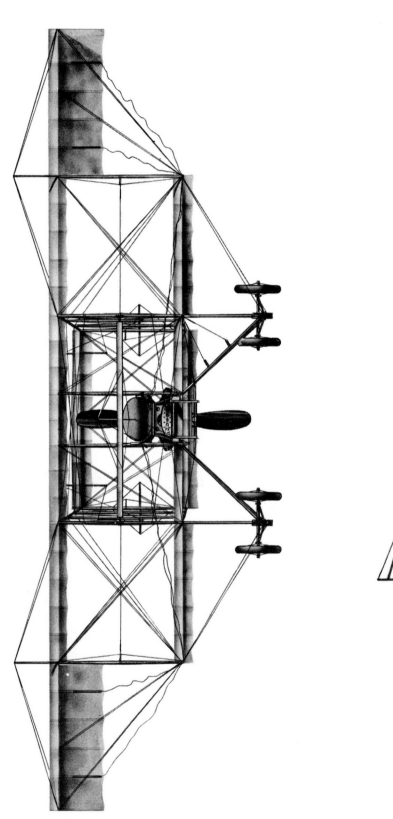

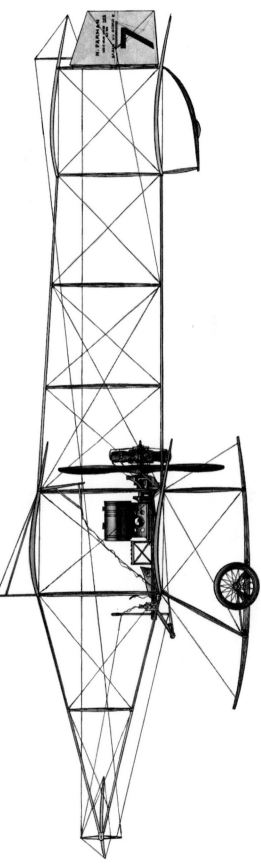

Nungesser's Nieuport scout

Charles Nungesser leans against the cowling of a Nieuport scout.

DUE IN NO SMALL PART to the efforts of Bleriot and the Farman brothers, though they were only among the leaders in a galaxy of great flyers and pioneer manufacturers, France from 1909 to 1914 became the world leader in aviation sport and aeronautical design and construction, and was in the forefront of the first tentative efforts towards the application of the aeroplane for military purposes. Early in 1910 a handful of French army officers began training as pilots and later that year some thirty aeroplanes were in service and double that number on order. Soon French military pilots were venturing on longer cross-country flights, participating in army manoeuvres and developing the utility of the aeroplane in rapid reconnaissance and liaison.

Considerable expansion occurred during the next four years; regular air formations were instituted, a research and technical branch formed and military air operations conducted to good effect on active service in the North African colonies. By the outbreak of war in 1914 France had a well-organised air contingent of some 26 small squadrons, mainly of two-seaters, comprising about 145 first-line aeroplanes.

These aircraft and their counterparts in other embryo air forces abroad were not fighting machines in the accepted sense. Although prior to 1914 bombs had been dropped and photographs taken from the air, machine guns and other armaments fitted to aeroplanes, and bombsights, gun interrupter mechanisms, airborne wireless and other military paraphenalia invented and tested, there was much theory but little practical experience of how to use the aeroplane to best effect; its destructive potential was only dimly foreseen.

During the great fluid land battles that characterised the first weeks of the First World War the aeroplane rapidly revealed its value in reconnaissance. To discourage the surveillance and the occasional missile from above, anti-aircraft ground armament rapidly developed and eventually the rival airmen began serious attempts to harrass their opposite numbers when encountered in the air, taking aloft all kinds of armament from pistols, rifles and grenades to the occasional machine gun.

Perhaps the first efficient fighter plane (as distinct from the fast scouting single-seater) operating in significant numbers was the Fokker E I

Nungesser's Nieuport 24bis as depicted in the general arrangement drawings.

single-seater introduced by the Germans in mid-1915. By using a simple mechanical inter-rupter linkage a fixed machine gun mounted on top of the nose decking could fire between the revolving propeller blades without hitting them. Instead of a pilot or observer struggling in a battering slipstream to manipulate and aim a heavy free-mounted weapon, the Fokker pilot crouched down in the cockpit, sighting along the barrel of the gun and aiming the whole aeroplane straight at his target, with a decisive improvement in accuracy and effectiveness. A comparatively few Fokker machines, using revised tactics and aerial evolutions to exploit the fixed forward-firing gun, wrought havoc over a period of months among the increas-ing numbers of Allied bombing, artillery-spotting and reconnaissance planes.

The Allies had no immediate effective answer to the 'Fokker scourge' except a small French single-seater Nieuport, the Type 11 or 'Bébé', introduced into service at about the same time as the Fokker. The Nieuport's weapon, usually a lightened drum-fed Lewis machine gun, was mounted on top of the wing pointing slightly upwards to fire forward over the revolving propeller and the butt could be hauled down by the pilot enabling him to change the ammunition drum or fire upwards into the belly of an adversary.

In every respect except its armament the Nieuport 'Bébé' was superior to the Fokker E I; it

Nungesser seated in a Spad single-seater fighter.

The fragility of the Nieuport Type 11 Bébé is emphasised in this picture of a crashed example.

was some 15 mph faster (97 mph top speed), climbed more quickly, was far more agile and manoeuvrable and had a higher operational ceiling. As quantities became available and were issued to the *Escadrilles de Chasse* it went far towards eliminating the Fokker monoplane threat. British single-seat equivalents, the D.H.2 'pusher' and Sopwith Pup biplanes, did not appear at the front until February-November the following year, and meanwhile Nieuport 11s were supplied to the Royal Flying Corps and used also by Belgium, Italy and Russia.

The following year a slightly larger, faster and strengthened Nieuport, the Type 17, appeared in time to counteract the introduction of the German Halberstadt and Albatross biplane fighters. Further refinements of the design to appear in the next twelve months included the Type 17bis with Clerget engine and Types 24, 24bis and 27 (usually with le Rhônes) with rounded rear fuselage sides, various engine powers and on some models revised tail surfaces and ailerons.

All these Nieuports had a common sesquiplane wing arrangement. The top wing was of generous area and set well down towards the pilot's eye level so as to restrict his forward and sideways vision as little as possible, while the lower wing was a small narrow plane minimising restriction of the downwards view; this surface gave little additional lift but by means of Vee interplane struts reinforced the top wing structure. The result was a better outlook from the cockpit than in conventional biplanes, with fewer blind spots to hide stalking enemy aeroplanes. The drawback was a certain lack of structural rigidily which is said to have resulted in structural failures in flight. Nevertheless, so compact and agile were the Nieuports that they continued favourites with many flyers even when the faster, heavier and stronger Spads became available.

The machine illustrated in the general arrangement drawing is almost certainly a Nieuport Type 24bis (no precise list of Nieuport type numbers seems to have been authenticated and exact identification of machines in the later production series sometimes presents problems), one of the many Nieuports flown by the great French ace Charles Nungesser. His aeroplanes were almost invariably distinguished by the macabre personal insignia of a coffin, candlesticks and piratical skull and crossbones painted in white on a black heartshaped motif outlined in white. While some may have felt that in using such a provocative emblem he was tempting the fates—and indeed he

Nieuport 23 was similar to the Type 17 but with the single gun offset to starboard of the centre line.

survived an astonishing number of crashes, mishaps and accidents—he was probably superstitious, as were many airmen, since he always had his insignia painted on the planes he flew and there is some evidence that he even retained the same army acceptance serial number N 1895 on the tail of several different machines by painting it over and obliterating the correct number.

Like a great many of the early flyers Nungesser had a background of motor sport and racing and almost naturally gravitated towards the fresh thrills and dangers of flying. After a spell with the French cavalry in the early days of the war he transferred to the air force, and in April 1915 reported to his first operational squadron, VB 106, flying the cumbersome but rugged Voisin pusher biplane bomber/reconnaissance aircraft. Here he painted on the nose of his machine the black skull and crossbones which later featured in his personal insignia, and began a long series of personal mishaps by being shot down by ground fire, quickly followed by his first aerial victory which earned him a transfer to a fighting scout squadron.

In November 1915 he joined the new squadron, N63, flying Nieuport Type 11 single-seaters, and shortly afterwards began the remarkable fighting career which earned him 45 confirmed aerial

victories, several spells of detention for insubordination, a shower of citations and decorations and a shattered and wounded body which he drove mercilessly to the point of collapse. Surviving the war he continued an adventurous flying life, running a flying school for a time and 'barnstorming' in the United States where he even made a film. His last and fatal adventure was an attempted flight across the Atlantic from France to North America in the face of the prevailing winds. With navigator Captain Francois Coli, Nungesser took off early on the morning of 8 May 1927 in the single-engined Levasseur PL-8 biplane, named 'The White Bird' and carrying his heartshaped black insignia, and disappeared for ever over the wastes of the Atlantic ocean.

Nungesser's Nieuport 24bis dipicted here was powered by a 120- or 130-hp le Rhône rotary engine, noted for its light weight and reliability, and armed with a single Vickers machine gun mounted in front of the cockpit and mechanically synchronised to avoid hitting the revolving propeller blades as they passed in front of the muzzle. The fact that this arrangement slowed the rate of fire and possibly imposed additional stresses on the gun and ammunition feed mechanism may have contributed to the extraordinary tardiness of the

Seen at the Nieuport aerodrome near Paris and labelled Type 17, this machine appears to be the prototype of the Type 17bis or possibly 24bis.

An Italian Nieuport Type 27. Note the rounded tail surfaces and curved fuselage sides as well as the divided landing gear axle, as compared with the Type 17s in the background.

An Italian Macchi-built Nieuport 17. Nieuports were used extensively by the Italian air force.

Allied technical authorities in following the German introduction of such mechanisms. They were also slow to follow the German lead of adopting a twin-gun installation which doubled the single-seater fighter's firepower.

In tandem behind the whirling rotary engine were the oil tank and a 75.5-litre fuel tank giving a not over-generous patrol duration of 1¼ to 2 hours according to throttle setting. The fuselage had a conventional wire-braced spruce box girder structure based on four longerons with plywood formers/frames and metal tube tail extremity, fabric-covered except for a plywood bottom, plywood and composition board covering forward of the cockpit and an aluminium engine cowling. The top wing had two hollow spruce spars with internal stiffening splines, wire cross-braced and with a plywood-covered leading edge and generous aileron area. The narrow bottom wing had a single spar with thicker internal splines together with more extensive plywood at the leading edge to give extra stiffness. All wing and tail surfaces were fabric-covered. Dimensions were: span 26 ft 11 in; length 19 ft 3½ in; height 8 ft with tail trestled and airscrew horizontal; wing area 161.5 sq ft; the empty weight was 838 lb, the gross weight 1245½ lb. The maximum speed was 116 mph at sea level and 103 mph at 13,100 ft, the climb to 6500 ft took 5 min 40 sec, to 9800 ft 9 min 25 sec, to 13,100 ft 14 min 40 sec and to 16,400 ft 21 min 30 sec; the absolute ceiling was 18,200 ft.

This machine was silver overall with dull metal cowling and broad red, white and blue bands on all the wing upper surfaces and on the rear fusel-age decking. Tricolour ribands often decorated machines of the French aces but were accentuated in this case because of an unfortunate episode Nungesser experienced in May 1917, when he was attacked by a British single-seater which appears to have mistaken the skull and crossbones insignia on the sides of his Nieuport for the black German crosses. Such an error was the more understandable because a close German copy of the Nieuport, the Siemens-Schuckert D-I, was used in small numbers by several German squadrons at about this period. The mistake was fatal for the British pilot, for having taken evasive action and had his machine peppered with machine gun bullets, Nungesser finaly assumed from his adversary's persistence that he was a German pilot flying a captured machine, rounded on him and shot him down. Landing beside the wreck in order to discover the identity of his opponent, Nungesser was horrified to discover from papers in a pocket that the dead airman was indeed British. Apparently to avoid a similar occurrence Nungesser had his Nieuport painted with the broad tricolour bands.

After this Vee-strutter series Nieuport developed more conventional biplane fighters, but after the war, when metal construction with its advantages of improved structural efficiency came into general use, Nieuport's designer Gustave Delage reverted to the sesquiplane layout for a series of fighters for the French air force, undoubtedly because of the comparatively unobstructed field of view from the cockpit. The wing arrangement finally became obsolete when fighters turned almost universally to the classic low-wing monoplane formula which persists to this day.

F

E

E

F

FEET

0   5   10

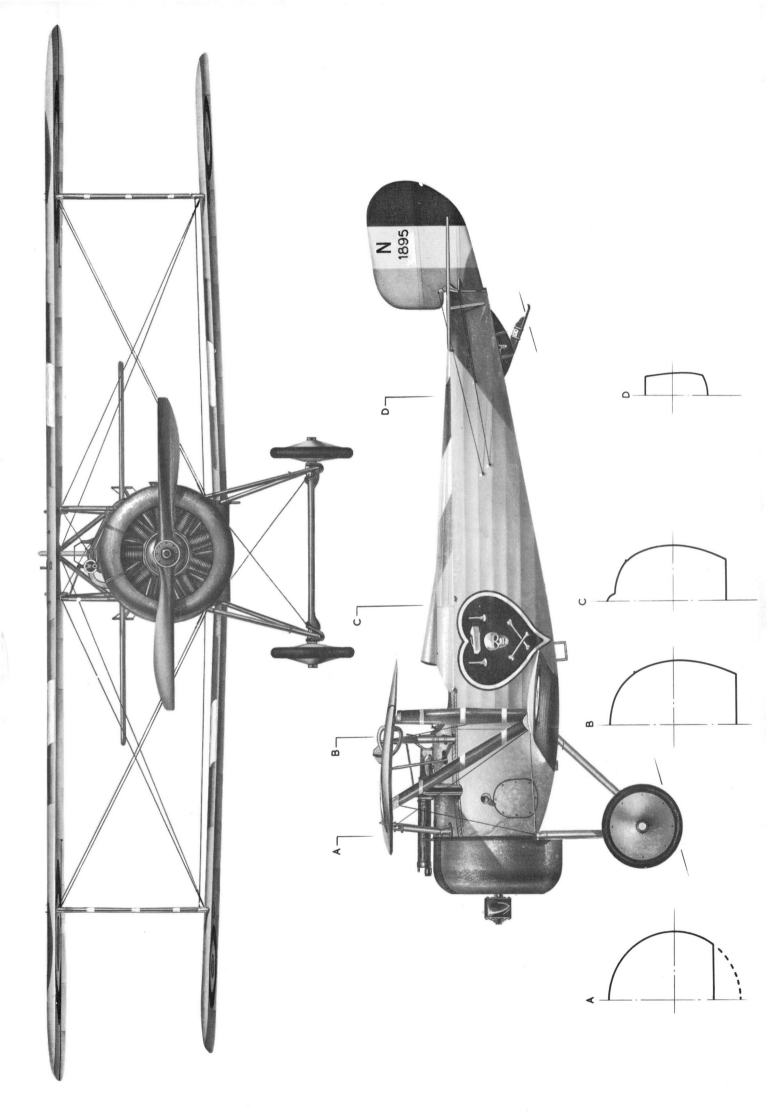

Guynemer's Spad SVII

A formal portrait of Georges Guynemer.

SOME OF FRANCE'S FINEST aeronautical engineering brains were behind the famous Spad SVII fighter, the prototype of which flew in April 1916. Directing the whole project was Louis Bleriot of cross-Channel fame, who headed a business group which had acquired the Deperdussin concern before the war and altered the one name, *Société Provisoire des Aeroplanes Deperdussin,* to *Société Pour l'Aviation et ses Derives.* Heading the airframe design team was Louis Bechereau, creator of several outstanding pre-war Deperdussin designs. Probably because of their prohibitive cost, the very advanced Deperdussin monocoque construction techniques were not repeated on his Spad single-seaters. Instead, calling on interim experience with the ingenious but impracticable A2 two-seater, Bechereau evolved a more orthodox but immensely strong and structurally 'dense' airframe with several interesting technical features.

The engine mounting was a wood and metal 'cradle' cantilevered out from the fuselage proper. The portions of the longerons adjacent to the wings were of extra heavy section and were joined together by stout uprights from which the centre section struts were extended upwards to support the top wing. The whole formed an exceptionally rigid truss supporting the wings, engine, fuel, armament and the pilot's seat and controls. The top wing was brought well down near the pilot's eye-level for the best vision forwards, but visibility upwards and to the sides was not so good because the cockpit was right beneath the trailing edge, from which a large 'bite' had to be removed to extend the view and enable the pilot to get into the cockpit. This necessitated a slightly unusual wing structure in that the 'rear' spar had to be pushed well forward to allow for this cutout and a third, auxiliary spar provided on which to hang the ailerons and stiffen the trailing edge. The wings were very thin, but rib spacing was extra close for stiffness and the biplane 'box' was well trussed with stout brass-bound interplane struts and heavy -section bracing wires, doubled up in places. The top wing centre-section was left free for the engine cooling system header tank and a small between-spars fuel tank. The main fuel tank was ingeniously shaped to form the belly of the fuselage beneath the lower wing.

The airframe was certainly one of the more interesting of the First World War period, and married to it was an engine of quite outstanding merit, the Hispano-Suiza 8A designed by the Swiss engineer Marc Birkigt. This was a V-8 unit of compact overall dimensions considering the power potential, with monobloc aluminium castings for each cylinder bank.

The French certainly needed a new fighter late in 1916. The agile Nieuport 11 sesquiplane had been more than a match for the Fokker monoplanes, and the Nieuport 17 for the Halberstadt and early Fokker biplanes. But in September 1916 the great Oswald Boelke led into action a picked band of pilots flying the formidable new Albatros D-I and II, which because of their two-machine-gun armament and excellent performance made as much of an impact on Allied air operations as had the Fokker Eindeckers. The Nieuports were outpaced and outgunned, though their agility prevented them from being completely outclassed.

The first two Spad SVIIs went to the front in that same month, September, the second of them going to Lieutenant Georges Guynemer, one of the most experienced and brilliant pilots of *Escadrille 3* of the crack French Stork group—GC 12, *Les Cigognes*. Guynemer's slight, boyish figure and tender years—he was nearing his 21st birthday—belied a ferocious and brainy fighter who combined the traditional dash and daring of the French with an intellectual and scientific approach to the problems of air combat. He made a study of the good points and blind spots of enemy machines, working out his own tactics to take advantage of the weak points of each. He corresponded regularly with Louis Bechereau about technical improvements for the Spad, and suggested the fitting of a 37-mm cannon between the cylinder banks of the Hispano. The Spad SXII Ca.1 was the result, armed with one Vickers machine gun and the 200-hp Hispano-Suiza 8Bc *moteur-canon*. Guynemer impatiently awaited the first example of his 'magical' aeroplane, and when it arrived shot down four enemy planes with it. But the disadvantages were great. The cannon was a single-shot weapon, demanding great accuracy at point blank range to secure a hit, and recoil and vibration problems were present. It had to be hand loaded in the midst of combat, which was distracting to say the least, and cordite fumes almost asphyxiated the pilot. The twin-Vickers installation of the Spad SXIII being developed at the same time was thought to be the more effective armament for the average pilot, and comparatively few of the cannon Spads were made.

Guynemer was the idol of the French public, the more so perhaps because of his obvious youth. He certainly had a superb fighting record: 54 confirmed victories, 600 aerial combats in just over

Guynemer in one of his Spad SVIIs, labelled Vieux Charles.

A Spad SVII of the famous Stork Group—Les Cigognes.

A British-built example of the Spad SVII. Note the Lewis gun mounted on the top wing.

two years at the front and more than his fair share of narrow escapes. Inevitably, constant fighting took its toll of his mental and physical stamina, though never of his courage, and finally—perhaps needlessly—he met his death. With increasing urgency his superiors had urged on him a complete rest from combat flying; Guynemer alive was a living legend, a great morale booster for the French people; Guynemer dead would be a national disaster. Yet he persisted in remaining with his unit until, on 11 September 1917, he failed to return from a morning patrol. Apparently, his companion on the flight last saw him engaging an enemy machine over Poelcapelle, Belgium. No expected information or propaganda about his death was immediately forthcoming from the Germans. Later it was rumoured that the ace had fallen beneath the guns of an ordinary German squadron pilot. On being pressed, the Germans stated that he was buried at Poelcapelle, but no trace of the grave was found when that place was captured soon afterwards. Altogether, Guynemer's death remains a mystery; no-one knew or would tell about his fate.

The Spad SVII depicted here is one of two earlier Spads flown by Guynemer and is preserved today in one of the galleries in *Les Invalides,* Paris, with every appearance of retaining its original finish. Overall colouring is now a fairly dark shade of ochre but was probably lighter when the machine was new. Metal and wood panelling around the nose is slightly darker and subtly more orange than the doped fabric. The yellow ochre finish seems to have been standard on non-camouflaged Spads and almost certainly was an opaque protective finish and not a clear dope. The fuselage numeral '2' and the Stork emblem are light red. Reds and blues in the tail stripes and wing roundels are distinctly lighter in shade than

current today: this applied to French First World War machines in general and also to many British aircraft of the same period, certainly as far as the blue was concerned. Apparently there were variations in standard British cockade colours just as in the standard airframe finishes.

The red numeral '2' was carried on the starboard wing top as shown in the general arrangement drawing, and mirror reversal of the same numeral was in a similar position on the port top wing and may have been provided to be read clearly in a rear-view mirror for quick identification in combat. These and the fuselage numbers were 'shadowed' in black as shown on the drawing. The name 'Vieux Charles' was painted in black on the fuselage side below the cockpit coaming and exhaust pipe, apparently on the starboard side only.

Data for the SVII was as follows: span, top wing 25 ft 8 in, bottom wing 24 ft 10 in; top wing chord 4 ft 7 in, bottom wing chord 4 ft 2 in; length 20 ft 4 in; height 7 ft 2½ in; wing area 193.96 sq ft; track 4 ft 11 in; empty weight 1168 lb; loaded weight 1630 lb. Guynemer's Spad SVII S113 depicted, virtually a prototype, had a 140-hp Hispano-Suiza 8A engine which attained a top speed of 109 mph with a ceiling of 16,400 ft. First production series machines had the Hispano-Suiza 8Aa of .150 hp at increased rpm, a top speed of about 112 mph and a ceiling around 17,000 ft, while the second production series had higher-compression 8Ac motors of 180 hp, raising the top speed to 122 mph at 6500 ft and the ceiling to 18,375 ft at 1665 lb loaded weight. This model climbed to 6500 ft in 6 min 40 sec, to 9800 ft in 11½ min and to 13,120 ft in 19½ min. Standard armament was one synchronised 7.6-mm Vickers machine-gun.

Top: *British-built SPAD SVII.*

Centre: *Another view of a British-built Spad SVII.*

Below: *The delicate frame of a tough fighter. Lieutenant Georges Guynemer stands in front of his Spad* Vieux Charles. *Note the tubular gunsight in front of the windscreen.*

35

O   5
FEET

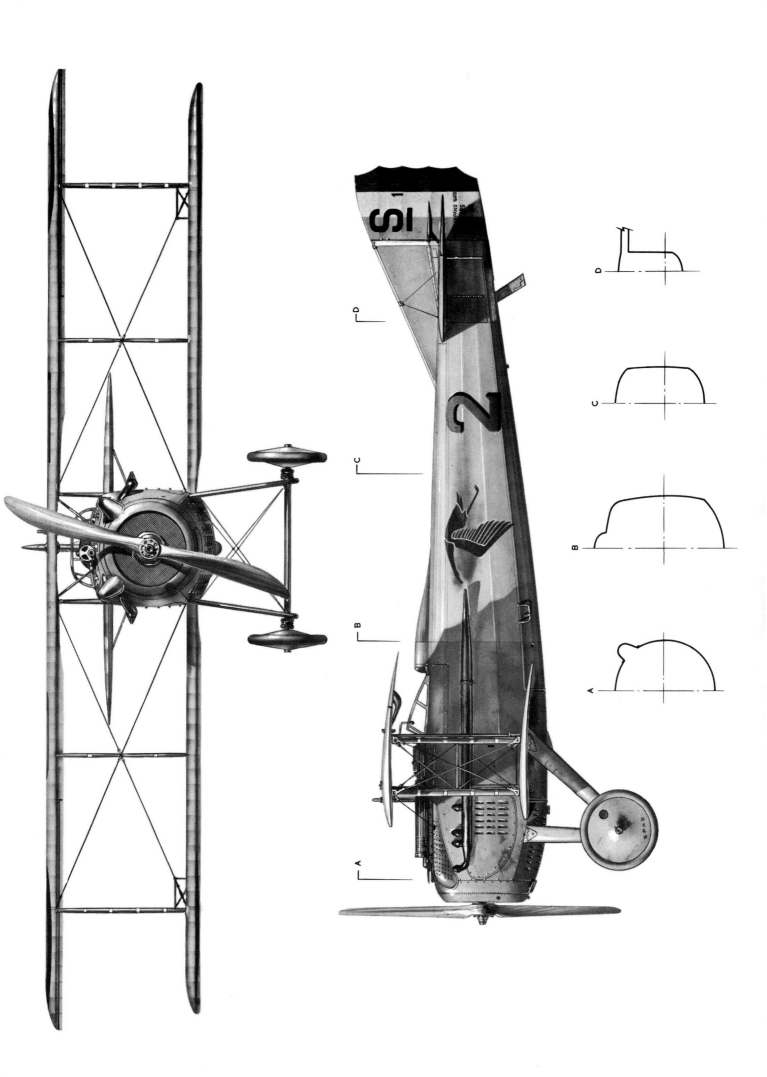

Richthofen's Fokker triplane

A portrait of Rittmeister Manfred von Richthofen.

RITTMEISTER MANFRED FREIHERR VON RICHTHOFEN was one of Germany's greatest 1914-18 air aces, top scorer with a confirmed tally of 80 enemy machines. Courageous, chivalrous, a deadly marksman, with steel nerves and a dedicated sense of duty to the Fatherland, he was also an avid collector of trophies from fallen machines, had a thirst for honours and decorations, and presented himself with a little silver cup, suitably inscribed, after each victory—foibles which no doubt diverted his mind from the dangers experienced every day in the air.

It was said by some of his former adversaries that he lacked the offensive dash of the great Allied aces, most of whom perforce had to penetrate well into the enemy lines to find their opponents. On the other hand, the German air service was nearly always generally outnumbered and into it was inculcated the idea that to live to fight another day for the Fatherland was more practical, and more in the line of duty, than to be killed in a fight to the death against impossible odds like the great Werner Voss. As a fine soldier and a hard but fair fighter, therefore, Richthofen was entirely successful even though he did not perhaps command the same universal recognition from the RFC as a man after their own heart as did Voss.

Manfred was made to follow in his father's footsteps as a soldier, the outbreak of war in 1914 finding him a Lieutenant in the 1st Uhlan Regiment. Transferred to the Western Front he witnessed the grinding of the war to a bloody stalemate and the carnage of Verdun. All the verve and glamour of the proud Uhlan Regiment had faded. He was a human mole like the rest, and like many other restless and energetic fighters his eyes turned skyward. In May 1915 he obtained a transfer to the flying service.

Richthofen saw action first as an observer and then as a two-seater pilot on the Russian and Western fronts. A hunter of wild animals in his native forests since childhood, his first quests for human game were frustrating. Not only was it the exception even to get near an enemy plane at that state of the war, but the crude armament and sluggishness of his machines made a kill difficult, though he did get two unconfirmed

The Fokker V4, one of the prototypes which led to the production Fokker Dr I.

victories, one as an observer and one as a pilot.

The great Boelke, at that time the war hero of Germany with 18 hardwon victories to his credit, had been sent on a tour of the war fronts to assemble picked pilots for one of the first regular fighting *Staffel*—and incidentally to prevent him suffering the same fate as the top-scoring Immelmann who had died on 18 June 1916. On the Russian front Boelke saw Richthofen (still a two-seater pilot) among others, and selected him to join the proposed *Jagdstaffel Nr. 2*.

Richthofen arrived at Lagnicourt to join *Jasta 2* on 1 September 1916. The unit received a mixed bag of equipment, mainly Albatros D IIs and Fokker D IIIs, and on its first offensive outing, 18 September 1916, Richthofen gained his first confirmed victory, over an RFC FE2b. With the crew mortally wounded, the FE fluttered to the ground, Richthofen making a rough landing nearby to examine his victim. He arrived in time to help lift the wounded airmen from the cockpits and lay them on the ground to give what aid was possible. The observer died almost immediately, the pilot later on the way to a dressing station.

The next day Richthofen visited the graves of his fallen opponents, placed a stone on each as a mark of his respect, and stood at their feet silently for a moment. He could not know that these were

the first of many, that more than 130 enemy airmen would go down killed, wounded, or captured beneath his guns; that his confirmed score would be 80 planes before the sands of his life, too, would run out.

In the next few weeks he shot down a Martinsyde scout, an FE2b, a succession of BE12 single-seaters, and then more FE2bs, a BE2c, and another BE12. On 23 November 1916 came a red-letter day for him when after a protracted combat he defeated and kills the crack RFC flyer Major Lanoe G. Hawker, VC, DSO who was flying a DH2 pusher fighter.

In a popular account of his fight Richthofen makes of it a personal duel with the English ace. In fact there were at least three other German machines with Richthofen, and what they contributed to the victory is not known—although in the early stages of the duel anyway it seems they kept clear of the arena. Of the four 24-Squadron DH2s that set out on the fateful patrol, two retired with engine trouble before they were engaged and a third retreated with battle damage, leaving Hawker to fight it out alone. He had made for Richthofen, and according to the latter's account there developed a prolonged bout of circling and jockeying for position, during which the combat was drifting on the prevailing wind ever further

Manfred von Richthofen poses with his brother Lothar beside a Fokker Triplane.

A factory photograph of a Fokker Triplane just off the production line.

into German-held territory. There came the moment when because of shortage of fuel or ammunition Hawker had to break off the fight and streak for his lines, showing his vulnerable tail to the faster German machines. Zig-zagging wildly to put off his pursuer's aim, Hawker sped towards home, but luck and Richthofen's good aim were against him. He received a stray bullet in the head and his machine crashed while still on the German side of the trenches. Hawker's single Lewis gun was sent back to Richthofen's home at Schweidnitz and remained perhaps his most prized trophy.

Manfred had his full share of good luck during his fighting life. He missed death by inches from a French shell, spun out of control in the smoke column over a blazing Russian village, nearly thrust his hand into the propeller arc of his twin-engined bombing plane near Dunkirk, and barely avoided a forced landing in Russian-held territory (where he would probably have received short shrift from the Russian infantry whose lives the German air service had been plaguing). During a combat on 9 March 1917 his machine was hit in the engine and fuel tank, but he managed to get to the ground unharmed.

Then, after raising his score to 57 victories, on 6 July 1917 in a fight with some FE2ds of 20 Squadron RFC, his head was creased by a bullet when (according to the FE's crew) he was making a head-on attack. An inch lower and that bullet would have killed him. As it was, temporarily blinded and paralysed by the blow, he spun down out of control. The rush of air revived him: he recovered his wits sufficiently to make a fair landing and, half unconscious, fell out of the cockpit into a patch of thorns.

A grimmer Richthofen started his scoring slowly after returning to the 'circus', *Jagdgeschwader Nr. 1* comprising *Jastas 4, 6, 10* and *11,* commanded by the Baron since late June. Nevertheless, he downed a further six planes before the year was out.

With each month at the front however the dice became increasingly loaded against him. His last victim, on 20 April 1918, was a Camel which went to the ground with the auxiliary fuel tank aflame, the pilot luckily escaping with minor burns from a crash landing. The next day Richthofen failed to return from his patrol. His machine had been seen to make a crash landing well on the Allied side of the lines.

The formation had encountered 13 Camels of Number 209 Squadron RAF led by Canadian Captain A.R. Brown, and during the course of the combat the Baron had streaked away to fasten on the tail of 2nd-Lieutenant W.R. May, an Australian out on his first offensive patrol. May's guns previously had jammed and he had spun out of the fight to make for home, followed swiftly by the watchful Richthofen. The first May knew of his pursuer was a spray of bullets zipping round his machine. All he could do was zig-zag frantically to avoid the deadly fire from behind (he afterwards joked that it was his bad flying that put the Baron off his aim).

Looking round during a brief respite in the battle, Brown saw his fledgling's deadly danger. Down went his nose in the wake of the weaving machines. According to his combat report he 'dived on pure red triplane' and 'got a long burst into him and he went down vertical and was observed to crash by Lieutenants Mellersh and

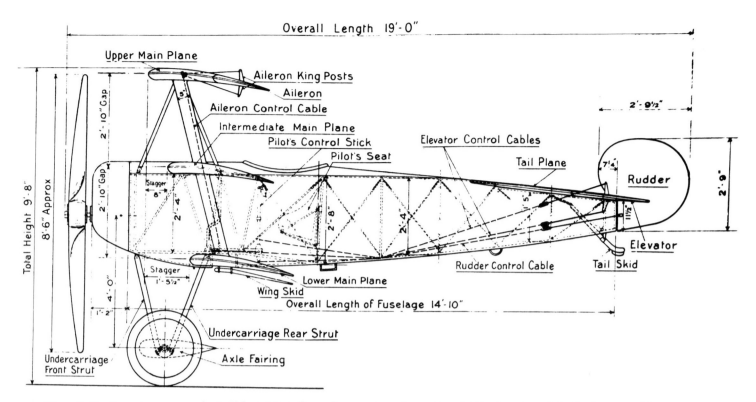

Overall Length 19'-0"

Upper Main Plane
Aileron King Posts
Aileron
Aileron Control Cable
Intermediate Main Plane
Pilot's Control Stick
Pilot's Seat
Elevator Control Cables
Tail Plane
Rudder
Total Height 9'-8"
8'-6" Approx
2'-10" Gap
2'-10" Gap
Stagger 8"
Stagger 1'-5½"
Lower Main Plane
Wing Skid
Rudder Control Cable
Tail Skid
Elevator
2'-9½"
2'-9"
Overall Length of Fuselage 14'-10"
Undercarriage Rear Strut
Axle Fairing
Undercarriage Front Strut

May. I fired on two more but did not get them.'

May and Richthofen had descended near to ground level, contour-chasing madly along the course of the River Somme. In doing so the Baron ran the gauntlet of ground fire from Austalian troops in positions below who saw the machine waver and shortly afterwards make a crash landing. Although Brown was later officially credited for the victory, rival claims were made on behalf of the ground troops who believed they had shot the Baron down. Exhaustive investigations then and to this day have failed to resolve the controversy.

The triplane featured in the general arrangement drawing shows as nearly as can be ascertained the Dr I 425/17 in which the dead ace crash-landed on that April day. The machine was reputedly all red except for the usual lightish blue undersurfaces (though the Baron's machines were not invariably coloured overall in this manner) with crosses outlined in white on the wings and fuselage, and probably a white tail with a plain black cross.

In designing the Dr I the Fokker team sacrificed speed for the rapid climb, small-radius turn and manoeuverability that the *dreidecker* layout could confer. The firm's association with Junkers resulted in the use of a thick, strong wing section using cantilever construction, which originally was intended to be stiff enough to do away with the usual bracing struts. In practice the structure was still weak and 'I' wing struts had to be added for production machines. Nevertheless, the Dr I still tended to shed fabric (and even its wings) in prolonged diving. Interesting points of the structure were the single deep box-spar with plywood rib-stiffened leading edge used in the wings, and the general use in the fuselage and tail

This dimensioned side elavation of the Dr I prepared by the British Air Technical Services shows the main structural features and dimensions.

The wreckage of the Fokker triplane in which Richthofen was shot down on 21 April 1918.

of welded steel tubes.

Engine usually was a 110-hp Oberursel (French rotary [Gnôme, le Rhône] built under licence) which gave a speed of about 115 mph near the ground and 80 mph at 18,000 ft. Typical climb performance was 3¾ minutes to 6560 ft and 14 minutes to 16,400 ft. Typical gross weight was 1260 lb and empty weight 829 lb. Records of dimensions vary, but the following were taken from a British Air Technical Services drawing dated 27 May 1918 and obviously based on measurements taken from a captured machine. Span, top wing 23 ft 6 in, middle wing 20 ft 6 in, bottom wing 18 ft 10 in; length 19 ft (tail up); height over top wing, tail up, 9 ft 8 in; airscrew diameter about 8 ft 6 in; wheel track 5 ft 3 in.

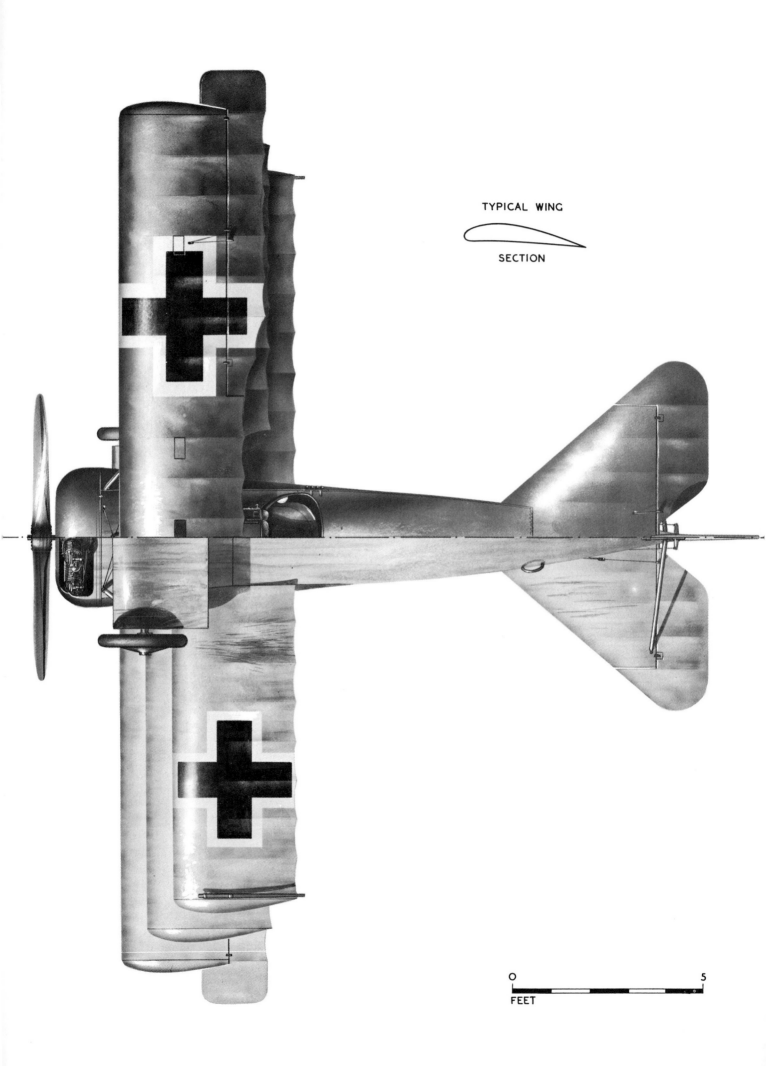

TYPICAL WING

SECTION

O   5

FEET

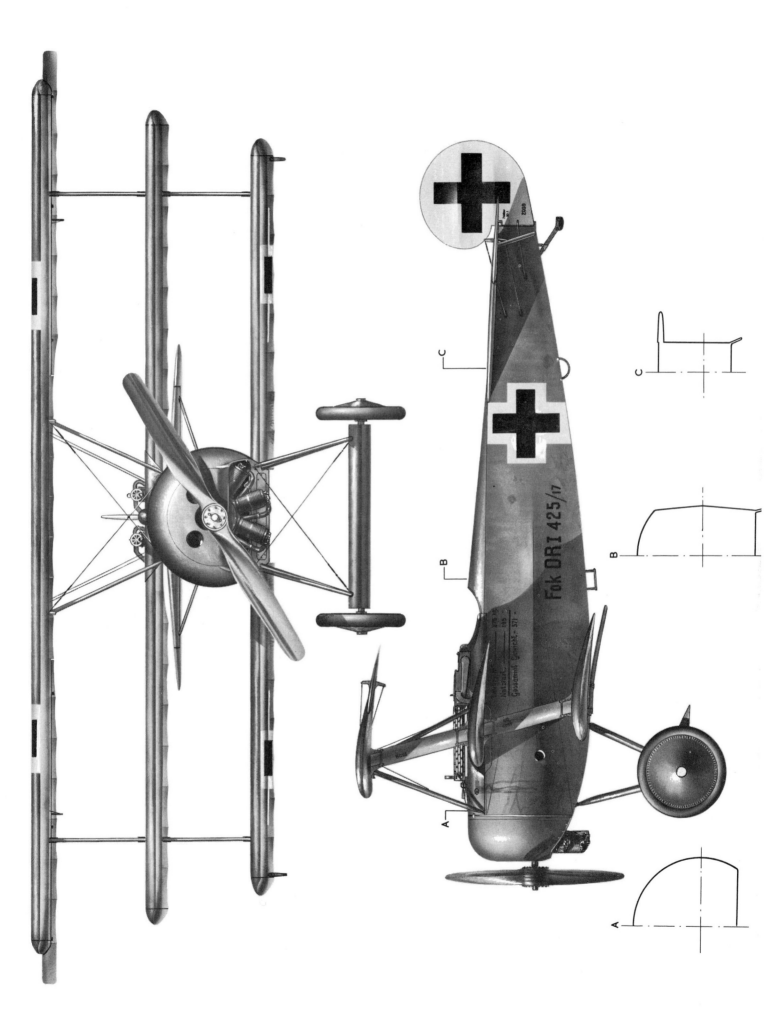

Major Barker's Sopwith Camel

THE FAME OF Major William George Barker,VC, much decorated Canadian First World War ace with 53 confirmed victories, rests on his epic single-handed combat with a whole German 'circus' of about 60 enemy machines on 27 October 1918. Barker took off in his personal Sopwith Snipe that morning to fly home on leave, but the sight of a high-flying two-seater over the lines which he took to be a German temporarily made him forget the comparative peace of England. He quickly climbed within range of the enemy and shot it down in flames. As he craned his head over the cockpit coaming watching the plummeting, flaming wreck-age, he was attacked by an enemy single-seater whose burst of fire wounded him in the thigh. Despite the agony of a shattered thighbone, he whirled the Snipe round after the German and quickly sent him down in flames.

Now, however, Barker found himself the target for a sky full of enemy planes. In the unequal combat that followed Barker was badly wounded twice more but sent several German aircraft down out of the fight. By now the Snipe was shot almost to pieces; Barker was practically unconscious with pain and loss of blood, and finally man and machine were forced to the ground, crashing just inside the British lines.

Incredibly, Barker survived this legendary combat, for which he was awarded the Victoria Cross, only to die twelve years later in a peacetime civil crash.

Barker's Snipe battle was the tailpiece of a remarkable fighting career as a single-seater pilot during which his mount was usually the redoubt-able Sopwith Camel. Originally a machine gunner with the Canadian Manitoba Regiment and acknowledged as a marksman, Barker transferred to the RFC as a gunner-observer late in 1915. Confined to the observer's seat, his aggressiveness nevertheless earned him the Military Cross and the chance to train as a pilot. At first he flew two-seater BE2cs and RE8s with 15 Squadron, and even with these ineffective reconnaissance machines managed to shoot down an enemy plane.

In September 1917 he at last got a transfer to a scout squadron, Number 28, forming in England

Major W. G. Barker, V.C., standing by the Sopwith Camel featured in the general arrangement drawing.

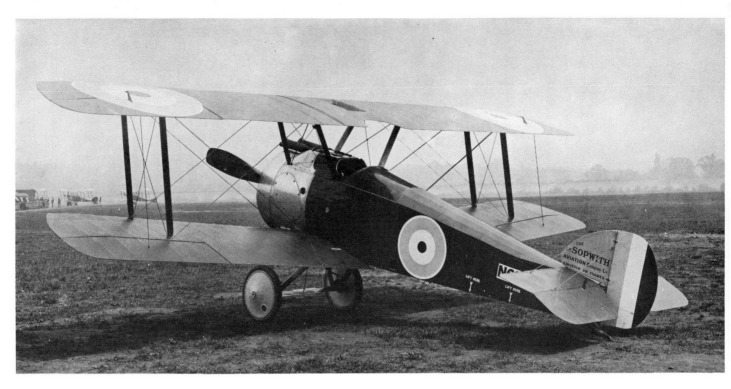

with Sopwith Camels. The Camel was the last of the new 1917 British fighters—which included the Sopwith Triplane, the Bristol Fighter, the DH5 and the SE5—to go into action, participating in the gigantic series of Passchendaele battles from the end of July 1917.

An obvious design progression from the beautifully balanced, agile Pup and the fast-climbing triplane single-seaters, the Camel had flying characteristics quite different from either. While the performance of early examples was hardly improved compared with the triplane, the Camel was more heavily armed with two synchronised Vickers machine guns to equate with contemporary German practice and had powers of rapid manoeuvre which in some respects bordered on the vicious.

Laid out in detail by designer Herbert Smith along general lines indicated by the managing trio at Sopwith Aviation Co. Ltd, T.O.M. Sopwith, Fred Sigrist and Harry Hawker, the Camel crystallised all the advantages of the typical British

A factory photograph of the Sopwith Camel with 110 hp Clerget rotary engine.

rotary-engined fighter. The light weight, compact power and short length of the French Clerget and Le Rhône and British Bentley rotary engines enabled the nose, and therefore the overall length, to be kept short so that power unit, armament, pilot and fuel weights were concentrated close to the centre of wing lift. Powerful leverage was exerted on this compact mass by generous tail control surfaces and 9 sq ft-area ailerons at all four wing extremities, with the result that the Camel immediately responded virtually to a touch; it could be stood on its tail, banked sharply or flick-rolled with the lightest pressure on the control column.

Strong torque reaction from the whirling rotary engine contributed its own peculiarities of handling

This 130 hp Clerget Camel has guns removed and a camera gun installed in their place for training purposes.

which, with the lightning response to control movements, made the Camel a testing and intimidating mount for the beginner and yet a superb fighting maching in the hands of a pilot who became familiar with and took advantage of its idiosyncrasies.

Simple and reasonably cheap to build, the Camel was manufactured in considerable numbers by many sub-contracting firms (some 5500 were made of the main F1 model) and employed on practically every fighting front as well as for home defence and by the British and United States navies.

Number 28 Squadron did not remain on the Western Front for long. The Italians had suffered a disastrous defeat on 24 October 1917 at Caporetto and were in headlong retreat. As part of British and French measures to bolster up the tottering front Number 28 and an RE8 squadron were sent to

Major Barker's Camel as illustrated in the general arrangement drawing.

Italy as the first British air reinforcement, and it was at the expense of German and Austrian pilots there that Barker began to build up his reputation.

Illustrated in the general arrangement drawing is Barker's personal machine, B6313, a fairly typical Sopwith-built example (powered as were the majority of Camels by the 130-hp Clerget rotary engine) which he flew in Italy with Number 28 Squadron and took with him when he was transferred to Number 66 and finally to Number 139 Squadron as commander. Account was kept of his mounting score of defeated enemy planes by painting the appropriate number of small white

This sectional view of the Camel highlights the compact grouping of engine, armament, fuel and pilot around the centre of lift of the wings.

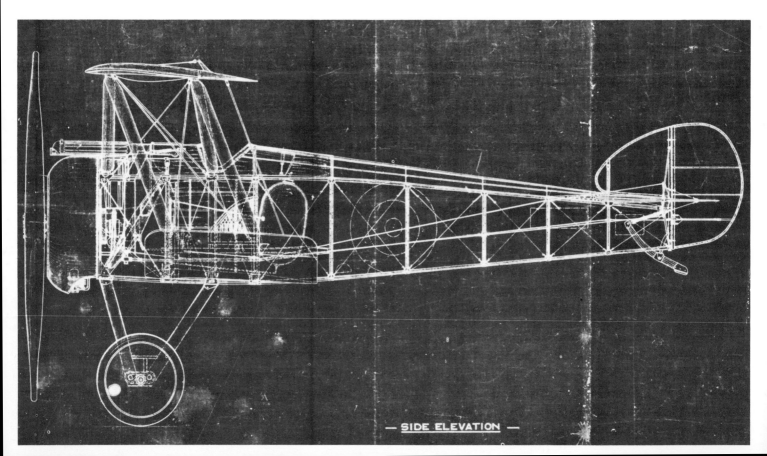

— SIDE ELEVATION —

An interesting photograph of a naval Camel poised on what appears to be a large lighter which would be towed behind a destroyer into wind for the aeroplane's takeoff.

bars on both wing leading interplane struts—37 can be counted in the accompanying photograph. Other special features of this particular machine were the arrow-pierced heart on the tail fin (a personal insignia), the white stripe squadron marking on the rear fuselage, the large portion of the top wing centre section stripped away to improve upward view and the additional cooling slots cut in the front of the engine cowling.

The basic colouring of the Camel varied in detail according to the production batch and the whims of the numerous sub-contracting manufacturers, but generally the upper fabric-covered surfaces were in varying shades of dark green-khaki and the bottom surfaces natural doped linen, the plywood areas around the cockpit being a darker shade of brown-green. The engine cowling and forward metal panels were a light French grey, khaki or, as on B6313, natural metal. Struts could be brown varnished wood or painted khaki with black-painted metal fittings.

The specification of a typical 130-hp Clerget-engined Camel was as follows: span 28 ft, length (tail up) 18 ft 9 in approximately, height (tail up) 9 ft approximately, upper plane area 125 sq ft, lower plane area 115 sq ft, track 4 ft 8 in, gap at

fuselage 5 ft, dihedral on top plane nil and on bottom plane 5 degrees. Maximum speed was 112.5 mph at 10,000 ft and 106 mph at 15,000 ft, climb to 6500 ft took 6 min, to 10,000 ft 10 min 35 sec and to 15,000 ft 21 min 5 sec, the service ceiling being 19,000 ft and the endurance 2¾ hours. The loaded weight was 1482 lb of which 532 lb were accounted for by the military load, pilot and fuel.

The battered Snipe, successor to the Camel, flown by Major Barker, V.C.

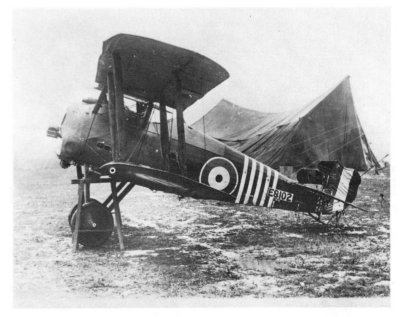

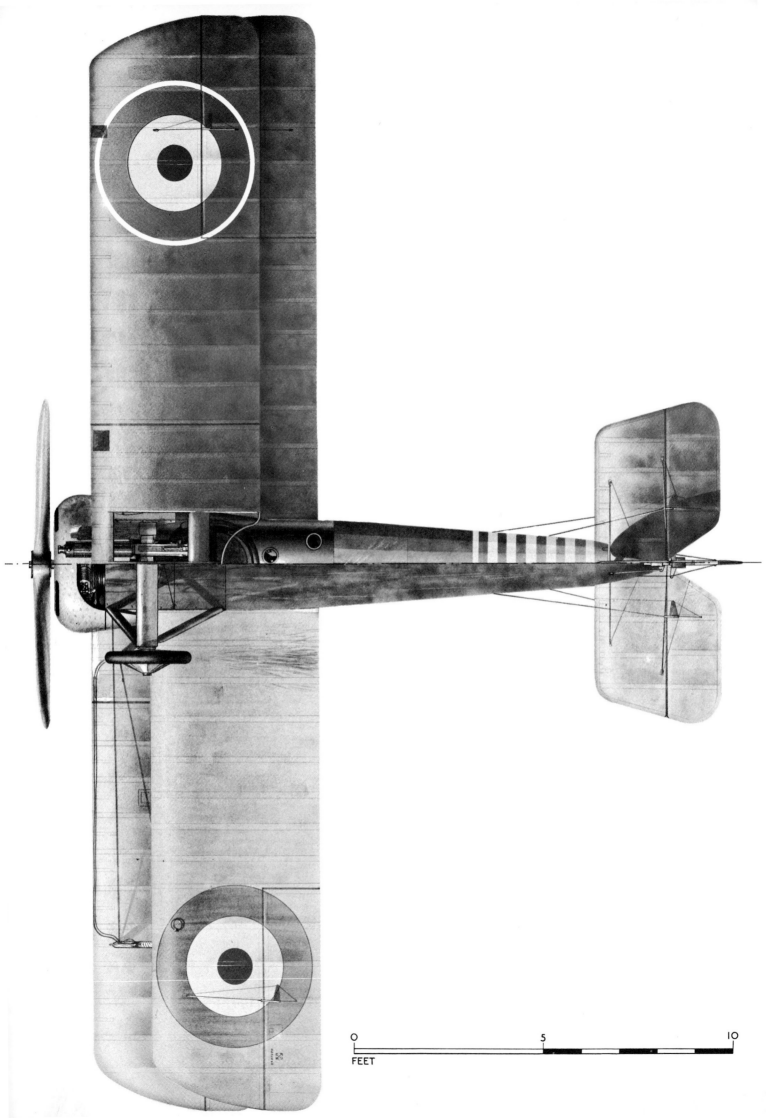

O   5   IO
FEET

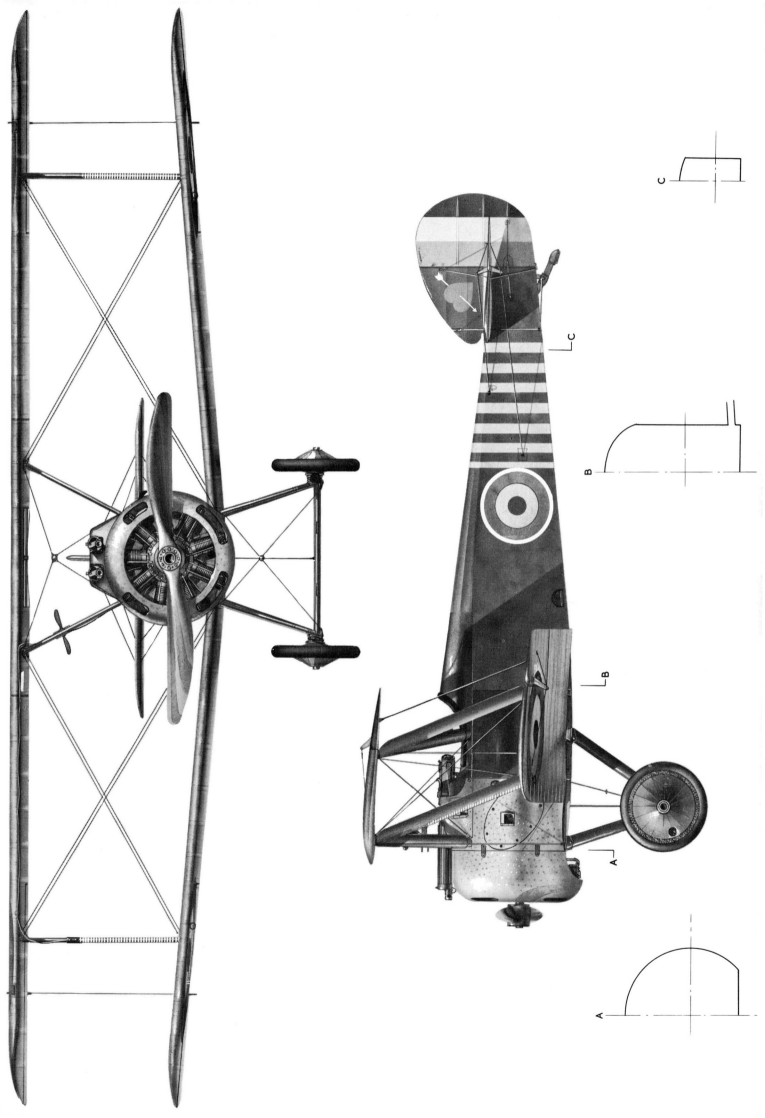

The Fokker D VII

IN A FEW SHORT MONTHS of service between late May and the Armistice, 1918, the Fokker D VII established an amazing reputation as a combat aeroplane. In January 1918 the prototype had won the first fighter competition held at the Johannisthal Aviation Centre near Berlin, in opposition to designs by Rumpler, Albatros, Pfalz, and L.F.G, one of the rules being that all competitors should use the 160/180-hp Mercedes engine. The new machines were put through exhaustive testing by some of the crack front-line pilots, whose unanimous opinion was that the D VII was the superior machine, whereupon it was put into large scale production not only by Fokker but by the Albatros firm and its Austrian subsidiary. Albatros since August 1916 had supplied the best German fighters of the period, the D I, II, III, V and Va. It was a bitter pill for them to swallow, first to loose the competition and then to have to manufacture their rival's product under licence.

Around 800 D VIIs were in action by August 1918, and Allied pilots found it a tough proposition. The best contemporary French and English single-seaters were the Hispano-powered Spad S13, which did between 130 and 135 mph according to the engine fitted; the 137-mph Wolsely Viper-engined SE5a; and the 121-mph Bentley Camel. The D VII did from 117 mph to 124 mph low down, again according to the motor fitted, and climbed to 10,000 ft in 12 minutes with the Mercedes, or 8½ minutes with the BMW. According to the official figures, therefore, it was slower at best than the Spad S13 or the SE5a, and only marginally faster than the Camel or even the two-seater Bristol Fighter. In the climb to 10000 ft with the Mercedes it was inferior in varying degrees to all three Allied single-seaters mentioned, but with the BMW it was better than the SE5a and the Camel, and slightly better than the Spad S13, the poor climb reputation of which is not borne out by the available figures. Statistically, the BMW D VII's ceiling of 22,900 ft was only fractionally better than the three Allied fighters.

Statistics can however be totally misleading, especially when applied to such an intangible subject as fighter performance. The D VII obviously had quite exceptional handling qualities,

borne out by its reputation for being extremely easy to fly even by a novice, coupled with a capability for lightning manoeuvre, and particularly fine flying qualities at extreme heights. Height then as now was the critical factor in air combat. The man on top always had the advantage, and it was the D VII's ability to get above its opponent that probably contributed most to its fighting reputation.

The French tested captured D VIIs extensively and issued the following figures after the Armistice for a machine with a Mercedes engine giving 180 hp at 1500 rpm and 184 hp at 1600 rpm. Top speed was 117.5 mph at sea level, 116.8 mph at 3280 ft, 114.3 mph at 6560 ft, 110 mph at 13,123 ft and 74 mph at 19,865 ft. The climb to 16,400 ft took 26 min (other reliable times often quoted are 31 min or even 38.5 min).

Nominally of about the same rating as, and obviously based on, the Mercedes, but built by Bayerische Motoren Werke, the 185-hp BMW apparently produced a quite different set of figures, the top speed being quoted as 124.3 mph at sea level and the climb to 16,400 ft slashed to 16 minutes, a reduction far outside the usual tolerances permissible between different production examples of the same type. Weights for the BMW version were 1516 lb empty and 1997 lb loaded. Dimensions were: span 29 ft 2½ in, length 22 ft 10 in, height 9 ft 8 in, wing area 217.3 sq ft.

Turning from the performance aspect, there can be no doubt about the advanced structural features of the D VII. The fuselage framework consisted of a light welded-tube metal structure, and the wings were thick-sectioned wooden cantilever assemblies with no internal or external wire bracing which could be shot away in combat and weaken the structure. The whole airframe dispensed almost entirely with the careful re-rigging required periodically by practically all other aircraft of the period, and obviously the D VII could face a considerable amount of battle damage without its structure collapsing.

The machine illustrated here is one of those flown by Ernst Udet—Germany's second-ranking First World War ace with 62 confirmed victories—when he was with the Richthofen *Jagdgeschwader*. He joined this unit on 26 March 1918 and was

Ernst Udet and the Fokker D VII featured in the general arrangement drawing.

British pilots examine a captured Fokker D VII

The Fokker D VII

Another Fokker D VII in Allied hands, the photograph possibly taken on a captured German aerodrome or after the Armistice.

quickly put in command of *Jasta 11*. As far as can be ascertained from photographic evidence, this particular machine had the entire fuselage sides and top, part of the fin, and probably the top of the horizontal tail surfaces painted the JG1 shade of red. On the fuselage side was the monogram 'LO!' in white, the initials of his fiancee which Udet painted on most of the planes he had flown. The rudder and a portion of the fin were white. There are reports of blue tails, candy-striped top wings, and white stripes on the tailplane, but this machine almost certainly was less decorative, with the usual printed fabric camouflage on the wing, fuselage

A Fokker D VII tested in the United States after the First World War.

and tail undersurfaces, the top surfaces being a darker shade. There were at least three basic printed fabric patterns used on German fighters at that time, a four-colour combination and two five-colour combinations in varying shades of buff, blue and green, mauve and violet, and pink and indigo. In the four-shade pattern shown on this D VII the colours possibly were dark blue, a light violet, buff, and sage green.

Udet was a very different personality to Richthofen. Sensitive, fun-loving, Udet's nature revolted from the daily blood-letting of friend and foe. After the war, he embarked on a colourful career as an aerial adventurer which took him all over the world until the 1930s, when he was persuaded to join the new *Luftwaffe* and quickly reached high office in the technical department. His work there has been criticised, but a most valuable contribution to Germany's war effort was the backing he gàve to continued undercover work on new jet and rocket-powered planes, despite

Hitler's orders that such work should be shelved in favour of all-out production of existing types. This was at a time, the autumn of 1940, when a great many people in Germany and elsewhere were still anticipating an early victory for the Axis, and long-term projects were thought to be a wasted effort.

Many of the technical and planning difficulties which dogged the *Luftwaffe* from then on were blamed on Udet. He became a political scapegoat for Goering's misguided policies, sucked helplessly into the treacherous whirlpool of internal Party rivalries. In despair he finally took his own life.

BOTTOM WING ROOT

TOP WING C/C

0   5   10

FEET

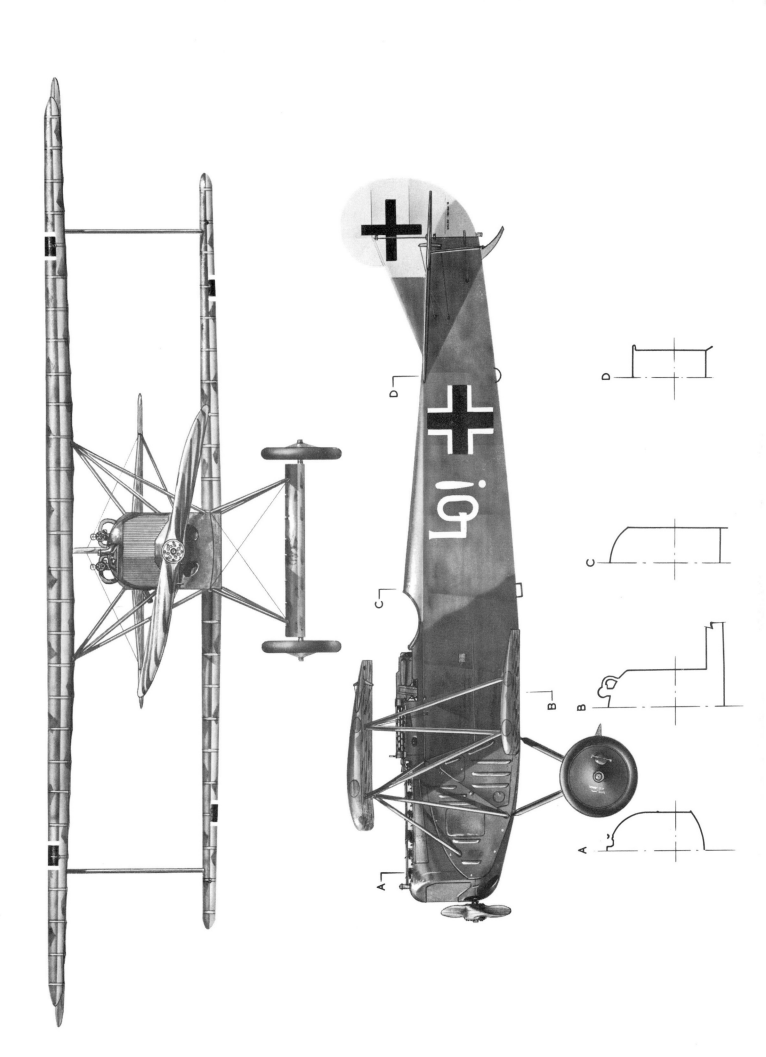

Hawker and Grieve and the Sopwith Atlantic

A wartime photograph of Harry Hawker.

AMONG THE GREATEST series of fighting scouts evolved during the First World War was that emanating from the Kingston-on-Thames works of the Sopwith Aviation Co. Ltd. And one of the chief contributors to the firm's rapid rise to fame and fortune from its formation in 1912, second only to T.O.M. Sopwith himself, was Harry Hawker.

Idol of pre-1914 flying-meet crowds, demonstrator of the early Sopwith products, closely involved in the design and testing of the great wartime machines, best known for his 1919 attempt to fly the Atlantic, Hawker has his name perpetuated in the trade name of another great fighter manufacturer, Hawker Aircraft, Ltd, now absorbed into the giant Hawker Siddeley Group.

Son of a blacksmith and wheelwright, Harry George Hawker was born in the small village of South Brighton, Victoria, Australia, on 22 January 1889. A reluctant scholar, he ran away from school for the last time when he was 12 to join an automobile firm, where he began the pursuit of his ambition to be an engineer. At 15 he was one of the best drivers in Victoria and became an expert mechanic and engineer.

When Hawker's imagination was caught by the growth of the embryo science of aeronautics, he began to cast around for the means to learn to fly. Prospects in Australia were virtually nil, so with a companion of like interests he sank his savings into a one-way ticket to England and opportunity. For nearly a year he progressed from one ill-paid job to another, and at one time considered returning to his own country.

Prospects of learning to fly seemed to be as far away as ever when one day he received a wire from a friend who had joined the tiny Sopwith Aviation Company saying there might be a place for him. Fred Sigrist, works manager at the time, found Hawker an expert mechanic and a hard, enthusiastic worker.

His craving to fly soon reached the ears of T.O.M. Sopwith, and so Hawker got his first lessons at the Sopwith Flying School at Brooklands. Soon he was instructing, among his pupils being Captain John M. Salmond and Major H.M. Trenchard, both to become famous service officers destined to reach highest rank in the Royal Air Force.

The Sopwith Atlantic

In charge of the Sopwith hangars at Brooklands, Hawker began his flying career in earnest. With only 20 hours flying time to his credit, he had several tries on the Sopwith/Burgess-Wright biplane for the British Empire Michelin Cup No. 1 duration record and £500 prize. A broken valve spring, high winds, and a rainsoaked magneto respectively brought the first and two subsequent attempts to premature conclusions, and on 24 October 1912, seven days before the competition was to close, he again failed after an early morning 20-minute flight because of magneto trouble. A brand new Bosch magneto was hurriedly fitted, but meanwhile F.P. Raynham had taken off with some difficulty in the heavily loaded Avro cabin biplane for a rival attempt.

Over an hour and a half later, the Sopwith machine was ready and Hawker took off with the A.B.C motor hardly warm. Anxiously, and then with mounting excitement, the Sopwith supporters watched the two machines steadily circling the drome in a gentle 5-8 mph wind. To save fuel and engine wear, Raynham hung the Avro on the propeller in an alarming manner, turning the least possible revolutions on the Green engine. Hawker's machine kept to a safer 400 ft height, its geared-down chain-driven twin propellers wafting gently around in contrast to the ABC engine's high-pitched buzz.

For hour after hour the two machines circled; then, just after 3 p.m., Raynham had to land for lack of oil. His 7 hours 31½ minutes flight created a new, though shortlived, British duration record.

Hawker was still circling steadily. Could he exceed Raynham's time? Minutes ticked by to the 1800 rpm buzz of the ABC. Nursing the fuel, Hawker dropped his tail lower and lower as he decreased the revolutions. A little knot of spectators began to gather around the timekeeper as he counted off the remaining minutes. One more circuit and Raynham's shortlived record would be beaten. Around came the Sopwith machine again, purring steadily, and a sigh from the crowd acknowledged the end of one record and the beginning of a new. Up went Hawker's tail and the machine pulled away on yet another circuit.

Hawker had a flask of cocoa, some chocolate and sandwiches aboard. He was quite cosy in the little streamlined nacelle. There were 32 gallons of fuel in the two tanks, more than enough for the flight as it turned out. Soon it was nearly dark, and Hawker opened the throttle fully and climbed to 1400 ft. The competition regulations stipulated that flying should not continue beyond one hour after dark, and at 5.50 p.m., just before the time limit, Hawker descended to look for the now-hidden landing ground. As he swooped low out of the night, officials on the ground lit gasoline flares in the nick of time to enable him to make a perfect landing, exactly 8 hours and 23 minutes after take-off.

His capture of the British Duration Record and the Michelin prize immediately brought Hawker into the forefront of British competition and record flying. On 31 May 1913 he took the Sopwith three-seat Tractor biplane (80-hp Gnome) to 11,450 ft to gain a new British height record. On 16 June he beat Geoffrey de Havilland's height

T.O.M. Sopwith examines the Sopwith Atlantic.

record of 10,560 ft with one passenger, reaching 13,400 ft despite intense cold. The same day, with a brief pause to thaw out, he took off again, this time with two passengers, to reach a record 10,800 ft. Finally, on 27 July 1913 he took up three passengers and reached 8400 ft.

Meanwhile, on 8 July Hawker had gained yet another success for Sopwith machines, winning the £500 Mortimer Singer prize for an amphibious aircraft. Six out-and-back five-mile flights and landings from a point on the land to one out at sea were made in the Sopwith Bat Boat.

Hawker made two unsuccessful bids for the £5000 *Daily Mail* Circuit of Britain competition of 1913. Entrants had to fly with a passenger a 1540-mile circuit of the coast within 72 hours, landing at various control points on the way. Hawker's first try on 16 August ended in his collapse from sunstroke and exhaust fumes shortly after landing at the Yarmouth control.

A second try, beginning on 25 August, got much nearer success. Starting from Southampton Water, the Sopwith seaplane touched down at the Ramsgate, Yarmouth, Scarborough, Aberdeen, Cromarty and Oban controls, as well as making several unscheduled stops in between for various reasons. The flight ended abruptly near Dublin when Hawker decided to land because of suspected broken valve springs. Spiralling down to the water, his foot (upon which oil had been dripping during the flight) slid off the rudder bar, and the machine

immediately sideslipped into the water. Had Hawker only known it, the Green engine's designer was waiting at Dublin with a new set of valve springs. The 1040-mile flight had taken 55¾ hours, or 21 hours 44 minutes actual flying time. As some sort of consolation, the *Daily Mail* presented £1000 to the Sopwith team.

Between competitions, Hawker was giving valuable assistance with the design and testing of machines like the Bat Boat and the three-seat Tractor. He also made a significant contribution to the design of the speedy Sopwith Tabloid, and piloted it on its sensational 90-mph debut at London Aerodrome, Hendon, on 29 November 1913, having that very morning made a 92-mph dash at the Royal Aircraft Factory, Farnborough.

A demonstration trip to Australia and more competitions and displays after his return to England preceded the First World War, during which Hawker did perhaps his greatest work, as Sopwith chief test pilot. Ill-health had dogged him for years and he was unfit for active service. On 4 August 1914, the day of the British declaration of war on Germany, he delivered his specially modified 'looping' demonstrator Tabloid to the 'Factory' at Farnborough. Thereafter he took a leading part, as one of the first designer-engineer-test pilots, in the development of the famous Sopwith wartime fighting aircraft. As one instance of his war work, between 13 July 1914 and 16 October 1916 Hawker tested 295 different aircraft.

With the war and a tremendous wartime reputa-

The Sopwith Atlantic showing the built-up rear fuselage which incorporated the boat.

tion behind them, Sopwiths turned with confidence (ill-founded as it turned out) to a civil outlet for their products. One of the new products was a Rolls-Royce Eagle-powered five-passenger cabin transport. When it was decided to enter a machine for the *Daily Mail* £10,000 competition for the first British-crewed machine to cross the Atlantic non-stop, the transport design was adapted as a special two-seater machine to be piloted by Hawker for an attempt. Sopwith entered their modified machine, named the *Atlantic,* on 11 March 1919, the machine having taken only six weeks to build. Fuel tanks replaced the original cabin and the open cockpit was arranged with side-by-side, slightly staggered seating to give maximum ease of movement and communication for the crew.

The motor fitted was the magnificent 360-bhp 12-cylinder Vee water-cooled Rolls-Royce Eagle, revving normally at 1800 rpm and consuming 24 gallons of fuel per hour at normal power. A two-bladed propeller was fitted later for the actual Atlantic flight.

Critics at the time abhorred the use of a single motor for such a long and hazardous oversea flight. Hawker's rejoinder was that hardly any multi-engined machine of the time could fly with full load with less than all its engines operating. If it lost one engine, then it would have to come down just as would the single-engined *Atlantic.* Also, the single-engined machine had a better height performance to rise above bad weather and navigate by the stars.

The *Atlantic* also featured a droppable landing gear which was to be released soon after take-off to cut down weight (by 4 cwt) and head resistance. Hawker figured that the risk of a belly landing—for which wooden skids were provided along the fuselage bottom—at the end of the flight would be more than offset by the improved fuel margin and the greater safety factor in an emergency sea landing, when a wheel undercarriage would dig into the water and somersault the machine.

The detachable top decking aft of the cockpit formed a small boat, complete with paddles, flotation bag, rations, flares, and a sea anchor. Rubber flotation suits of U.S. Navy pattern with inflatable air bags back and front were worn by the crew.

Current for the radio (which on the flight proved to be useless) was provided by a wind-driven generator, the propeller of which could be retracted into the fuselage when not in use.

Hawker was to take as navigator Lieutenant-Commander K. Mackenzie Grieve. The crated machine, attended by the fliers, left England on the SS *Digby* on 20 March 1919, bound for Newfoundland. Captain Montague Feen had gone on ahead with a ground party to find a suitable site for a flying field.

It took a week after their arrival at St. Johns on 28 March to assemble the machine in its specially constructed wooden hangar, and then the crew settled down to testing, and to wait for favourable weather reports. Each day the machine was groomed, the engine run up, and the water system carefully filled and finally emptied again to guard against freezing. The detachable boat and the immersion suits were tried out in the nearby lake, and experiments made with various radio installations.

Soon after the arrival, Hawker's old duration-record opponent, Raynham, turned up with the Rolls Falcon-engined Martinsyde Raymor and Captain Morgan as navigator, for their rival attempt. The faster Martinsyde was quickly made ready, and thereafter the two teams watched each other like hawks to guard against a surprise take-off. Days of bad weather went by, and tension mounted to such a pitch that finally the contestants came to a gentlemen's agreement to give due notice of an impending start. Throughout the rest of April and well into May, weather reports were adverse.

Meanwhile three U.S. Navy flying boats, NC1, NC3 and NC4, had taken off from Rockaway Beach and headed for Trepassey, Newfoundland, on the first stage of a trans-Atlantic air crossing. Hawker saw the likelihood of the honour of the first crossing, though not a non-stop one, falling elsewhere than to Britain. With the NC boats on their way to the Azores, he decided to take off at the earliest possible opportunity. A little later, on 18 May, weather reports being reasonable though hardly favourable, Hawker and Grieve decided to make their attempt.

At 3.15 p.m. (5.51 p.m. Greenwich time), with 350 gallons of fuel aboard and mail which included a letter from the Governor of Newfoundland to King George V, the *Atlantic* trundled down the slope on its take-off run, barely clearing the ditch and fence at the far end. Climbing away into the sunlight, Hawker glanced down to see Raynham's Martinsyde on the rival landing ground, surrounded by a crowd of people. At 1500 feet he dropped the undercarriage (the airspeed indicator immediately jumped forward seven mph) and passed over the coast, heading northeast.

Sea fog was encountered almost immediately, but Hawker was soon above this into a clear sky. Grieve had time to get a quick drift reading and the level fog-bank horizon was acceptable for sextant readings.

For the first few hours the sky was bright and clear, the plane cruising at an indicated 105 mph at 10,000 ft. But 400 miles out the weather began to close in and they were soon encountering thick haze and an occasional rain squall. An hour later, glancing at the water thermometer, Hawker saw that it read high despite his opening the radiator shutters to their full extent. Obviously there was some obstruction in the cooling system, and he thought back to their careful filling and emptying of the system back at Mount Pearl. Perhaps too much rust had formed during the process and was now clogging the water passages.

Cloud was now thick around and below them, preventing the taking of drift readings. Later they found that they had drifted 15 miles south of their intended course. Water temperature continued to rise, and eventually Hawker decided to try to disperse the obstruction by cutting the motor and diving the machine. The manoeuvre seemed to be successful for the temperature remained moderate as they climbed back to cruising height, but 60 minutes later, 800 miles and six and a half hours out from Newfoundland, the gauge had again crept up to danger level. Unless something could be done, the 17 gallons of coolant would slowly boil away and precipitate a forced landing in the sea. Further diving was of no avail, and the only remedy was to struggle to 12,000 ft and there cruise on the minimum throttle opening to save the water. The top wing centre section was covered with ice formed by the condensing steam, and a plume of vapour streamed back from the radiator vent.

By now the moon was well up, and Grieve got an occasional observation on the stars through the gaps in the cloud. For several hours Hawker managed to keep the coolant below boiling point, but 12 hours out, on the morning after their take-off, a solid range of fantastic black cloud peaks fully 15,000 ft high blocked their way. A long detour could not be risked, and so it was decided to go under the front.

Down they dropped with the motor stopped to lower the water temperature. Quite near the sea, Hawker opened the throttle—and nothing happened. Frantically Grieve began to pump up fuel to the carburettor, until Hawker slapped him on the head and yelled at him to brace himself for the crash. On the downward swoop the engine must have become stone cold because of lack of water in the radiator tubes and block passages. Barely ten feet above the wave tops the motor fired and Hawker banged open the throttle, the engine bellowed, and up they staggered from what would probably have been a watery end, into the eye of the rising sun.

This fright convinced the fliers that they would not reach Ireland, and it was decided to use the last hour or two of the coolant to search for a ship alongside which they could make a landing. For over two hours they flew a zig-zag pattern in worsening weather and fog, searching for a vessel.

The watch of the Danish steamship *Mary*, eastward bound, sighted the machine at about 7 a.m. Greenwich time on the morning of 19 May. Hawker had been almost overhead before he spotted her in the gloom. Circling, he fired off three Very light distress signals and then flew off two miles ahead to make a superb landing in heavy seas. The machine floated well but began to break up under the impact of the waves washing over it, and the fliers launched their boat in readiness to abandon ship. As they waited in the waterlogged cockpit, the *Mary* came up, but it was an hour and a half before one of the boats gallantly fought its way 200 yards to the sinking plane against mounting seas. With Hawker and Grieve aboard, the boat was hauled back by line to the *Mary,* but nothing could be salved then from the plane.

Back home in England the drama continued for a week. The *Mary* was without wireless and no word of the fliers reached home. They appeared to have been lost without trace. Obituary notices appeared in the press.

But on Sunday 25 May, the coastguard station at the Butt of Lewis, Outer Hebrides, wired to HO that they had been signaled by a passing Danish vessel. The fliers were safe aboard. The country went wild with relief and enthusiasm, and the progress of Hawker and Grieve from Scotland to London was something of a triumphal procession, ending with an audience with the King and Queen at which they were each presented with the Air Force Cross.

The pair had flown about 1050 miles at an average speed of 80 mph and had used only half their fuel when they were forced to land. Had the cooling system not become blocked, the probability is that the flight would have been successful, for the motor ran perfectly despite the overheating, and the weather, though threatening, was not impossible.

Raynham and Morgan never got off at all. Trying to get away before Hawker gained too much of a lead, Raynham attempted a take-off in an adverse wind, crashing the heavily-laden machine in the process.

The Sopwith team was awarded a magnificent consolation price of £5000 by the *Daily Mail,* but the main £10,000 prize which both crews had failed to win would not be unclaimed for much longer. For on 13 June 1919 a Vickers Vimy piloted by Captain John Alcock and Lieutenant Arthur Whitten Brown was waiting ready at St Johns to take off and head out over the Atlantic.

Contemporary sources vary slightly as to figures for the *Atlantic,* but Hawker himself gave the following: span 46 ft 6 in; overall length 31 ft 6 in; chord 6 ft 3 in; gap 6 ft; cruising speed, using 15 gallons per hour, 105 mph; maximum speed 118 mph; speed at 10,000 ft, 105 mph; ceiling, loaded for Atlantic flight, about 13,000 ft; maximum economical endurance 31 hours; all up weight 6150 lb; disposable load 3350 lb; engine, Rolls-Royce Eagle VIII, 360 bhp. Tail-up height, 11 ft 1 in; top plane area 280 sq ft; bottom plane area 255 sq ft; tailplane span 11 ft 4 in; propeller diameter 9 ft 6 in.

After the Atlantic attempt Hawker turned to automobile and power-boat racing as well as continuing his competition flying. The Sopwith Company became defunct, and the new Hawker concern was still making two-stroke motor cycles when Hawker's Nieuport Goshawk, which he was testing prior to participating in the 1921 Aerial Derby, caught fire in mid-air. Out of control it struck the ground and blew up, killing the pilot instantly.

These photographs illustrate how the rear fuselage decking was partially formed by a small boat which could be detached and launched to save the crew in the event of a forced landing in the sea.

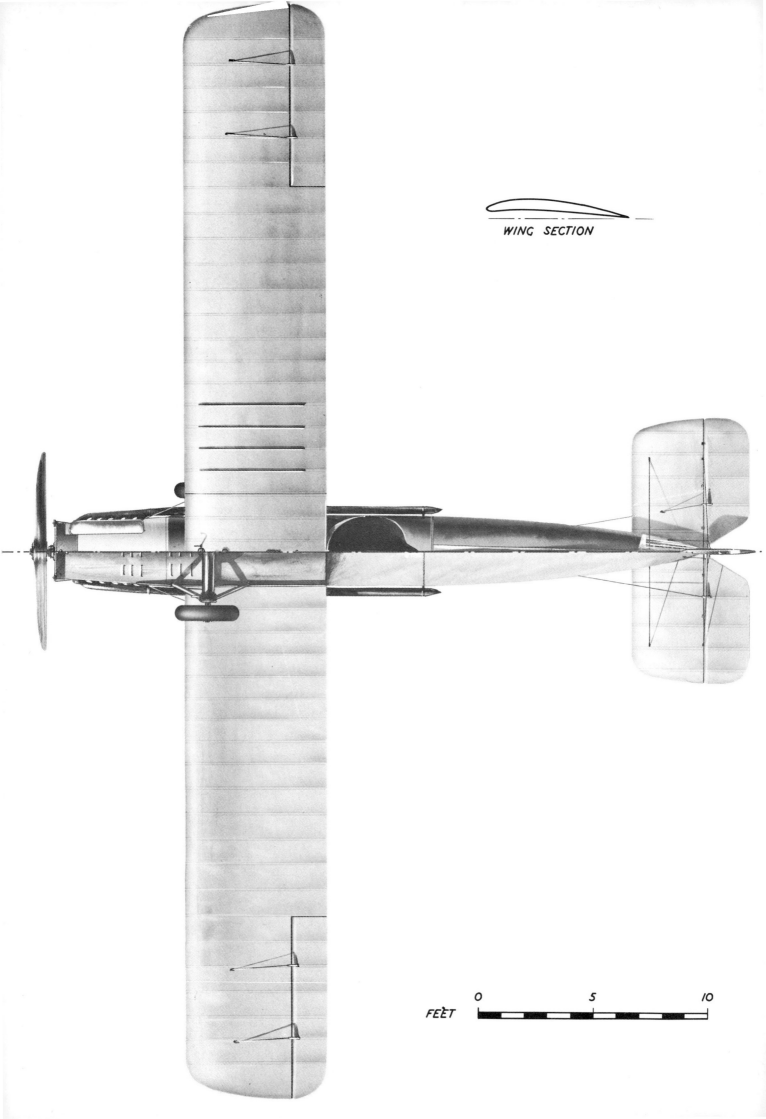

WING SECTION

FEET
0   5   10

General Pinedo and the *Santa Maria*

Francesco de Pinedo.

ITALY HAS PRODUCED her full share of great airmen and fine aeroplanes, one of her greatest fliers being General Marquis Francesco de Pinedo. Born in 1890, Pinedo had a naval training and served in the Italo-Turkish war and in the First World War.

Pinedo was struck by the great possibilities of the aeroplane as a postwar transportation medium, and also by what he deemed were the advantages of the flying boat for the long-distance transcontinental air travel he foresaw. Water was the perfect prepared landing medium, near all the great capitals and major population centres of the world. In the days before the long-distance airliner there was much to be said in favour of his arguments.

To prove his point Pinedo made a succession of air voyages spanning all five Continents. On his first major aerial argosy he set out from Sesto Calende in Northern Italy on 20 April 1925 in a small Savoia S-16 single-engined biplane flying boat, bound for Australia and Japan. The 6½-month flight to Tokyo and back earned him acclaim in Italy and a growing recognition as a navigator abroad.

Even more ambitious, involving crossing the South Atlantic and the vast Brazilian jungles, was his journey to the Americas and back in 1927. Mussolini gave the flight his blessing and suggested that it be extended into a goodwill tour of North as well as South America, ending with a return flight across the North Atlantic. Pinedo was to use an early example of the famous twin-hull Savoia S-55 flying boat and took with him Captain Carlo de Prete of the Royal Italian Air Force as relief pilot/navigator, and as mechanic Vitale Zacchetti, chief engineer with the Isotta-Franschini engine company. Taking delivery of the plane, named *Santa Maria,* at Sesto Calende they flew down to Cagliari, Sardinia, to take on fuel and equipment. Departing from there on a clear, bitterly cold Sunday morning, 13 February 1927, the plane headed out over the Mediterranean, skirting the North African coast, to Dakar and Bolama. There, just before take-off, they discovered a small black stowaway named Ali whom they had hired to clean and load the plane; it took all three of them to throw him off.

The next hop, from Dakar, was the hazardous one out over the Atlantic. After a preliminary stop at the Cape Verde Islands they started on the lonely 1450-mile ocean flight south-west to Fernando Noronha Island, off the Brazilian coast. Engine overheating and a near miss of a 1500 ft-high water spout were only two of the hazards they encountered on that trip. From there it was a brief three-hour journey to Natal on the mainland.

Equally as risky was the flight across the Brazilian 'big woods', the Matto Grosso, which the crew undertook after a tumultuous welcome in Rio de Janeiro and Buenos Aires. Following the rivers and lakes they conquered the 'green hell' and came out into more open country and down the great Amazon river, nearly 60 miles wide in places, to Para. Across the Guianas, skirting the Caribbean via Puerto Rico, Haiti, Cuba and the Gulf of Mexico flew the *Santa Maria,* finally reaching the mainland again at New Orleans to begin an extended tour of the United States.

From New Orleans Pinedo headed for California along the Mexican border country. But on the way, at Roosevelt Dam Lake, Arizona, on 6 April disaster struck and the *Santa Maria* was destroyed by fire. During refuelling, leaking fuel had spread across the water; someone carelessly dropped a lighted match and almost immediately flames engulfed the plane. Pinedo was ashore and his two companions directing the refuelling luckily escaped, but it seemed that having come so far their plans were now ruined. The American Government offered them a plane in which to continue the trip, and soon came news from Rome that a replacement Savoia was aboard a steamship bound for New York.

In the *Santa Maria II* they made another start from New Orleans, this time heading north to St Louis and Chicago, into Canada and across to Trepassey, Newfoundland, facing out across the North Atlantic. The fliers set off from this favourite trans-Atlantic jumping-off point bound for the Azores against strong winds. Fuel began to run out and 300 miles short of landfall Pinedo had to alight on the sea near to a Portugese vessel, which took the Savoia in tow in rising seas. Later the Italian steamer *Superga* took over the tow and brought the flying boat into Horta.

Sea damage repairs were effected there, the flight being resumed on 10 June eastwards to Lisbon, round the coast of Spain to Barcelona,

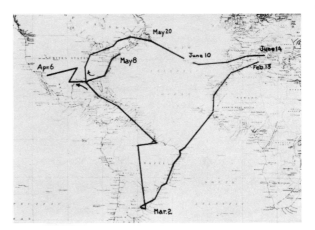
Map of de Pinedo's flight.

The Savoia-55 Santa Maria.

A military version of the twin-hull Savoia S-55

finally reaching Rome and a personal reception by *Il Duce*. For the 36,000-mile Four-Continent flight Colonel Pinedo was promoted to General as well as receiving international honours. Further flights might well have been undertaken but some trouble, probably political, occured in the background, Balbo stepped into the limelight, and Pinedo ended his service career as air attache in Buenos Aires.

That was not the end of his flying aspirations, however. After a lengthy period of preparation, on 2 September 1933 Pinedo was ready to take off from Floyd Bennett Field, Brooklyn, in the Bellanca *Santa Lucia* for a nonstop flight to Baghdad. But the overloaded plane never left the ground. Hurtling down the runway the machine began to swerve and plunged across the grass and through a fence to burst into flames. For some unaccountable reason all Pinedo's training and experience had deserted him at that most critical moment in his life, and he perished in the blaze.

The S-55 was designed by Mr Marchetti of *Società Idrovolanti Alta Italia* in both civil and military versions. Its special features were the commodious twin hulls, expected to make the plane especially seaworthy, and the thick broad wing, in which was the cockpit. Supported above the wing were two strut-mounted tandem Issota-Franschini 'Asso' 12-cylinder in-line water-cooled engines which gave a maximum output apiece of about 525 hp at 1900 rpm. The *Santa Maria* was equipped with sailing gear, a fresh-water distiller, fishing and mooring tackle, a collapsible raft, and carried 335 gallons of fuel in eleven tanks.

Data were: span 78 ft 9 in; length 54 ft 2 in; height 16 ft 5 in; wing area 1002.149 sq ft; maximum speed 127.4 mph; cruising speed on the flight averaged 100 mph; climb to 6560 ft took 15 min; to 9842 ft 32 min; ceiling was 13,123 ft; empty weight 10,141 lb; normal loaded weight 14,630 lb and maximum overland 17,936 lb.

This is Santa Maria II, *which replaced de Pinedo's first machine destroyed by fire on 6 April.*

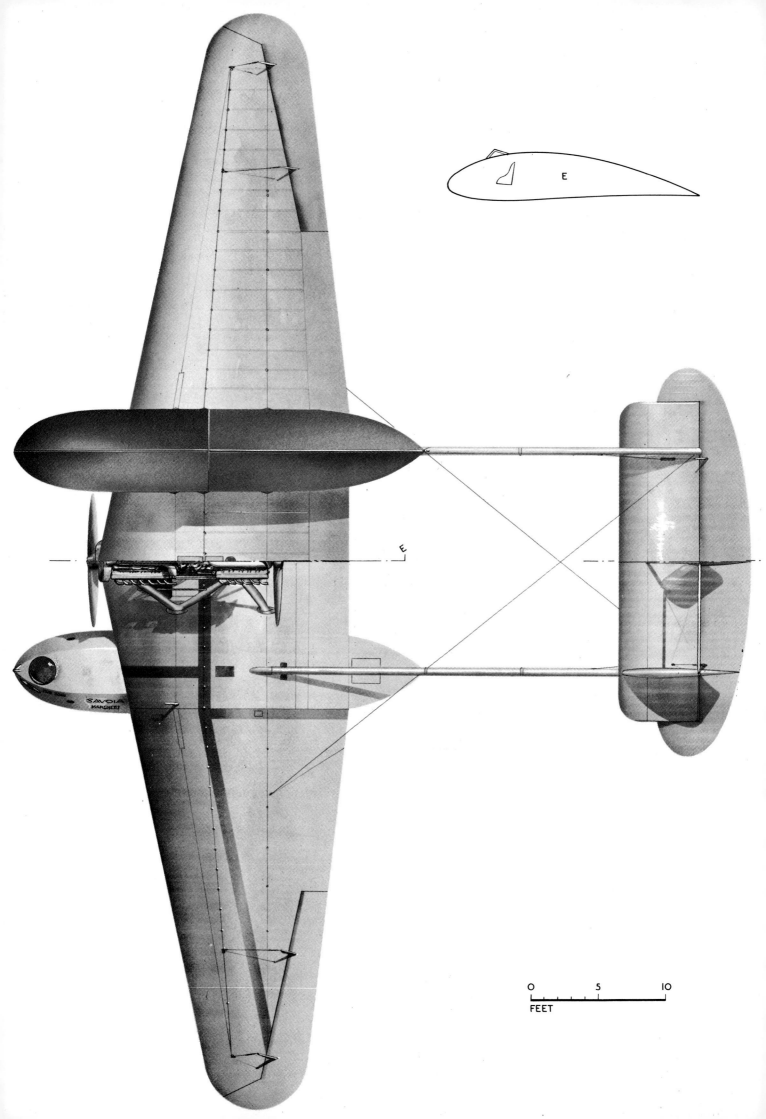

E

FEET

0   5   10

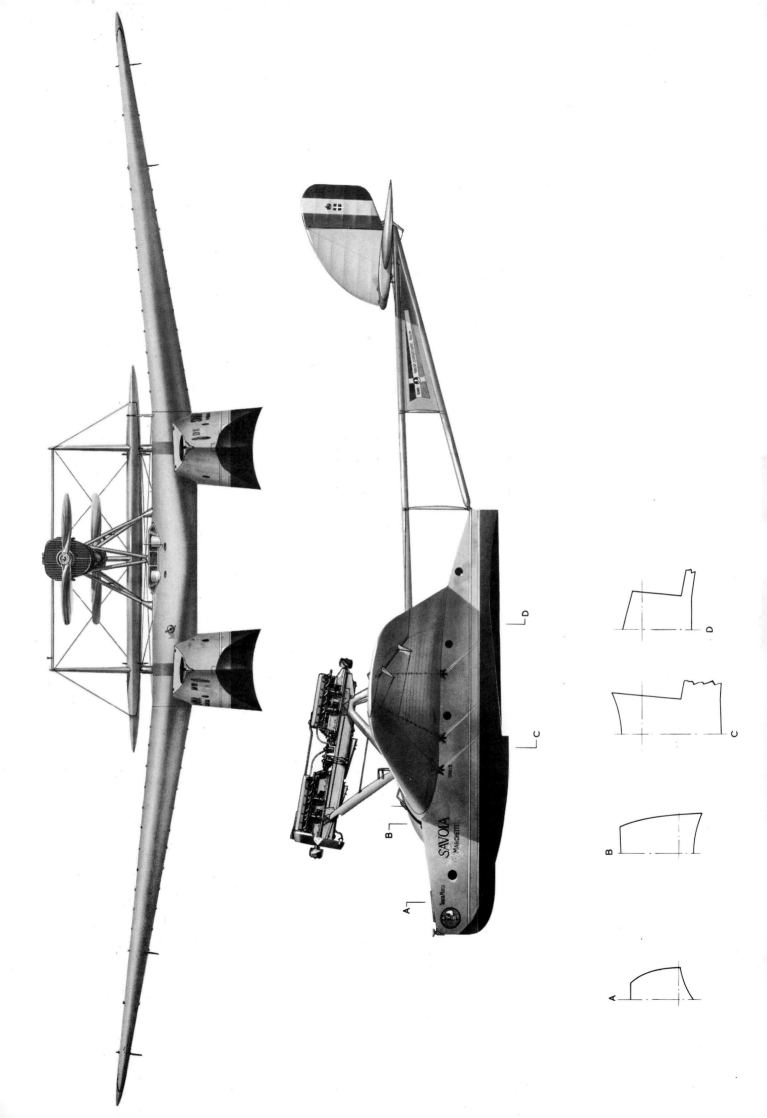

Left to right: *Mr. J.W. Stannage, wireless operator, Captain Saul, navigator, Captain Kingsford-Smith, leader and Captain Vandyk, pilot, standing in front of* Southern Cross.

'Smithy' and the *Southern Cross*

AS EARLY AS 1920-21 Captain Charles E. Kingsford-Smith and Captain C.T.P. Ulm were independently seeking financial backing in the U.S.A. and Australia for a proposed flight across the Pacific. Unbeknown to each other the two Australians, wartime pilots and now civilian fliers, nurtured the same improbable ambition. In fact they met briefly on one occasion and parted without either knowing what was filling the other's mind. Not until six years later did they finally discover that they were 'twin souls', upon which, adequate finance still eluding them, they decided to create interest by flying round Australia, a project for which it was much easier to get backing.

They did the 7500-mile trip in ten days five hours, creating a new record. At a triumphal luncheon in Sydney given by Sun Newspapers Limited, 'Smithy' and Ulm came out in the open with their trans-Pacific plan before an audience of prominent public and business men. The Government promised them £3500 and it seemed that other support would soon be forthcoming, so they both sailed for the USA to begin preparations.

First plans had centred around a Ryan plane such as Lindbergh used for his Atlantic crossing. There were nebulous ideas to fly the machine as a landplane from San Francisco to Honolulu and then fit floats for further ocean hops to Australia. This scheme was quickly shelved when in America they came up against the navigational and other problems involved, and the fatalities of the Dole Race to Honolulu confirmed them in the opinion that the margin of safety of a single-engine plane over the Pacific would be far too small. They also decided that the best possible radio gear was necessary to aid navigation and for emergency use.

Carefully they studied details of the planes and equipment used on recent long-range and Atlantic flights, comparing the wing and power loadings. It soon became apparent that the Wright Whirlwind engine and Fokker planes between them had by far the largest percentage of successes, and this combination they decided they must have. Almost immediately the chance to purchase a Fokker came their way. Sir George Hubert Wilkins telegraphed to say that he had a trimotor Fokker for sale without instruments and engines. The Whirlwinds, it seemed, would be more difficult to come by, for

Southern Cross is inspected by the public after its arrival in Australia.

Another photograph of Southern Cross *in later years with civil registration and a new paint scheme.*

Wrights were well behind with Government contracts for the engine and unable to fulfil civil orders immediately. Through the good offices of the navy, however, three engines earmarked for that service were made available instead for the Fokker.

Finance continued to be the bugbear, and in an attempt to raise funds 'Smithy' decided to try for a new world's endurance record, then standing at 52 hours 22 minutes 31 seconds (by Risztics and Edzard of Germany in a Junkers W33). There followed four unsuccessful tries, and then on 17 January 1928, stripped of everything essential—even the wheelbrakes—loaded up to over seven instead of the normal five tons gross weight, her tanks filled with 1522 gallons of fuel, the Fokker—now named *Southern Cross*—staggered into the air from Mills Field, San Francisco. 'Smithy' and Lieutenant G.R. Pond were at the controls, and they had to bump the Fokker into the air over a levee at the end of the runway. For 50 hours they circled San Francisco bay but at 10.13 a.m. on the 19th had to land, exhausted and out of fuel. Short of the record, without the expected prize money and completely broke, 'Smithy' and Ulm faced the prospect of selling their Fokker and returning to Australia.

At this low point in their fortunes they met up with wealthy Captain G. Allen Hancock, who later decided to buy the machine from them for £3200 and finance their flight in it across the Pacific.

After acquiring the engineless machine, 'Smithy' had had numerous modifications carried out to fit the plane for his purpose. Extra vertical structural members were inserted in the fuselage and the whole rear end stiffened to take the greater all-up weight. The wing held four 96-gallon tanks, another 107-gallon tank was put under the pilots' seats, and there was an 807-gallon main tank in the cabin—a total of 1298 gallons of fuel. Flexible fuel pipes were fitted to withstand prolonged vibration and the landing gear strengthened. Fuel from the main fuselage tank could be dumped in 50 seconds by means of a special 8-in diameter valve to lighten the plane in an emergency landing. Should they come down in the sea, the plan was to saw off the outer engines and the fuselage and use the plywood-covered cantilever wing as a huge raft, in which were carried rations and a small distilling plant for water.

With careful preparation and a complete plane overhaul at Douglas Aircraft, Santa Monica, full co-operation from the authorities and services, with three engines of proven reliability, powerful radio, and the wing raft, 'Smithy' and his companions felt they had reduced the risks of the proposed flight to sensible proportions.

It was with relief after the months of organisation that Kingsford-Smith and Ulm took off in the *Southern Cross* from Oakland Airport, San Francisco, on the misty morning of 31 May 1928. Behind them in the cabin were two Americans, Captain Harry Lyon, navigator, and James Warner as radioman. Heading out over the Golden Gate with 1160 gallons of fuel aboard, they settled down to the monotonous 2408-mile first lap to Honolulu, the sea blue below them and devoid of shipping, a blue vault above. They sighted land again the next morning at 10.52 a.m., and escorted by other welcoming aircraft descended into Wheeler Field, having averaged 88 mph for the 27-hour 25-minute crossing.

A photograph of Southern Cross *taken some time after the Pacific flight; the machine now bears the Austrailian civil registration VH-USU.*

The next leg was the longest, over 3000 miles to Suva in the Fiji Islands. 'Smithy' ferried the plane across to Barking Sands on neighbouring Kanai Island, where a 4500-ft runway more suitable than Wheeler Field for a full-load take-off had been prepared. The following morning, 3 June, they took off again and headed along the radio beam transmitted by Wheeler Field. This leg proved to be more eventful, with a threatened fuel leak that turned out to be condensation round the cold fuel pipes, the radio temporarily out of action, blinding rain squalls, a coughing starboard motor that miraculously soon cleared itself, and storms in their path which had to be skirted. But Lyon's navigation was masterly; they landed at Albert Park Sports Ground, Suva, at 2.21 p.m. (Pacific time) on 4 June, 3144 miles with less than 200 miles' fuel left in the tanks.

Take-off for the last and shortest hop to Brisbane was delayed because of the difficulty of transporting fuel to Naselai Beach, 20 miles from Suva. The wheels left this perfect runway at 2.50 p.m. on 8 June. Aboard they had a whale's tooth, a Fijian good luck charm presented to them by the oldest inhabitant, and as it turned out they needed it. The weather outlook was good, but soon after dark as they droned along visibility decreased to a mile, torrential rain began to drum on the

airframe, and strong gusts buffeted the plane. The whole night they ran the gauntlet of successive storms, barely keeping the machine in the air. Towards dawn the weather quietened, but the first grey light revealed a dank panorama of sullen sea and cloud. Nevertheless their spirits began to revive. Despite the failure of their earth inductor compass, Australia was a big target to miss, and Lyon's reckoning was that they were only a few hours out from their goal.

Landfall was made at Ballina, just south of Brisbane. They turned up the coast and glided down into Brisbane's Eagle Farm aerodrome at 10.13 p.m., having completed the 1795-mile stage in 21 hours 35 minutes at an average 83.5 mph. Between them and their departure point at San Francisco lay 7347 miles of ocean. The great Pacific had been spanned for the first time by air, the first and the greatest of many great flights by 'Smithy' and the *Southern Cross.*

The *Southern Cross* was an early example of the 'long span' Fokker F-VIIb-3m commercial monoplane. The plane is shown in the drawing as it was on the first Pacific flight in a colour scheme reported as light blue fuselage and vertical tail, and silver or gold wings. Later there were many detailed changes inside and out. A feature unique to the *Southern Cross* was the square-cut rudder.

Another view of the Southern Cross *taken several years after the Pacific Flight.*

Original data was as follows: span 71 ft 2 in; length 49 ft 9 in; height 12 ft 9 in; wing area 728 sq ft; wheel track 13 ft. Take-off weight from Oakland was 14,400 lb, the empty weight 5370 lb. Performance recorded on delivery tests at 11,000 lb gross weight was: maximum speed 122 mph; cruising speed 100 mph; landing speed 55 mph; climbing speed 720 fpm at ground level; service ceiling 12,500 ft. The Whirlwind engines were of J-5C type giving a normal 200 hp at 1800 rpm.

One of the world's greatest aeroplanes, the *Southern Cross* is preserved in a fine memorial hangar at Eagle Farm Airport, Brisbane, where she completed her first great long-distance flight. Unhappily she is the sole survivor of a great trio, for Ulm, and later Kingsford-Smith, were lost in attempted record flights before the war. But Harry Lyon and James Warner were able to attend the memorial inauguration at Brisbane in 1958.

FOOTNOTE: Most people for years have accepted, erroneously it seems, that the *Southern Cross* was a composite aircraft using the fuselage of the single-engine F-VII *Alaska* and the wings, tail, and landing gear of the tri-motor F–VII *Detroiter*, both machines originally bought by Sir Hubert Wilkins for Arctic exploration.

An Austrailian-owned Fokker airliner very similar to the Southern Cross.

Mr Gregory C. Kohn, in a brilliant piece of historical detective work published in a past issue of the American Aviation Historical Society Journal, seems to have proved conclusively that the *Southern Cross* and the original *Detroiter* are in fact one and the same plane, except for the engines and 'Smithy's' modifications. The main components of the *Alaska,* including the fuselage but less the wing which was wrecked and completely stripped, are on view at the Liberty Memorial Building, Bismark, ND.

F

0   5   10
FEET

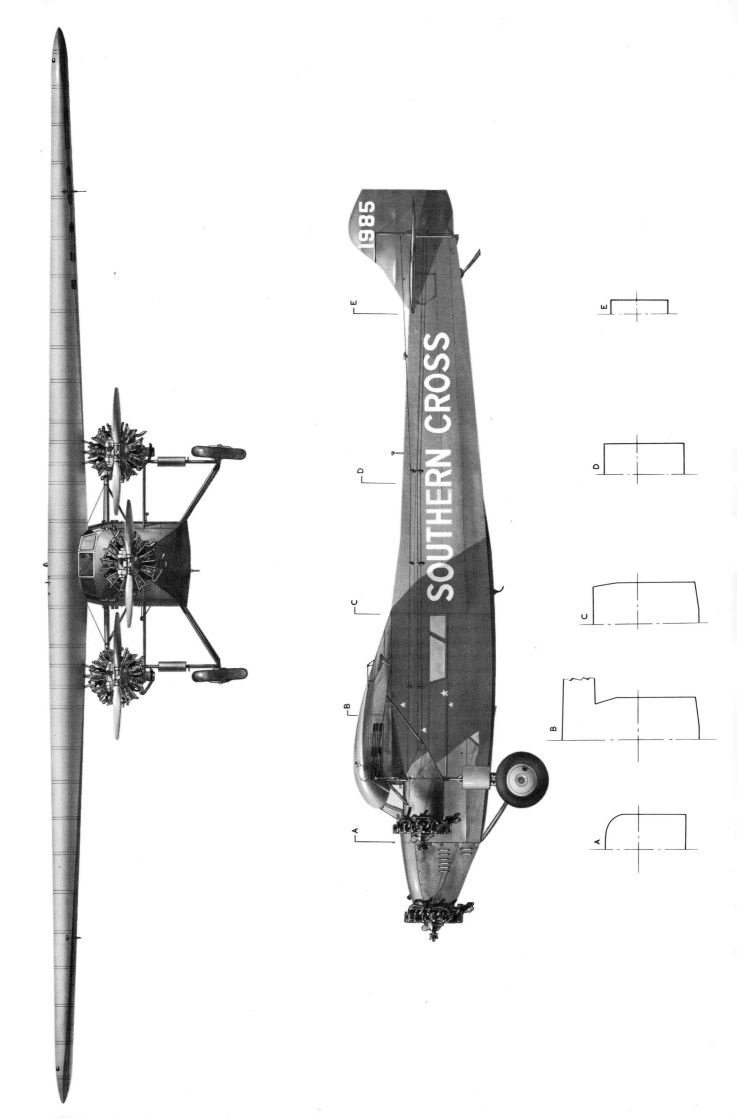

The Lindberghs' Lockheed Sirius

Charles Lindbergh

Above right: *A factory picture of the original Sirius Model 8.*

Below right: *The Lockheed Sirius landplane as featured in the general arrangement drawing. This photograph was probably taken on the Lindberghs' Los Angeles–New York flight of April 1930.*

CHARLES LINDBERGH'S epic first solo flight across the Atlantic in 1927 tends to overshadow the rest of a colourful flying career, in particular the far-ranging pioneering flights accomplished with his wife in the ensuing years.

After his triumphant return from Paris he turned down a flood of business offers and opportunities, donations and propositions of every kind. His first devotion was aviation, and soon he was touring the country in the *Spirit of St Louis* for the Guggenheim Foundation for the Promotion of Aeronautics, attempting to foster public interest in a bigger civil air programme.

Almost immediately after the three-month tour, 22,350 miles around the 48 states, he was off again on a 2100-mile, 27-hour 10-minute nonstop flight to Mexico City on the invitation of the Mexican president, Plutarcho Calles. After a triumphant reception at Valbuena Field, and Christmas at the home of Dwight W. Morrow, the American ambassador, Lindbergh flew off on a goodwill tour of the Central American Republics, made a spectacular flight across the Andes, a circuit of the islands of the Caribbean, and finally ended his two-month odyssey with another remarkable 1200-mile bad weather trip from Havana to St Louis.

Lindbergh had already met Anne, daughter of Dwight W. Morrow, in New York. During Lindbergh's several visits to Mexico between December 1927 and February 1929, their engagement was announced. Three months later, on 27 May, Colonel Lindbergh and Miss Anne Spencer Morrow were married at Englewood, NJ.

The same year, Lindbergh took delivery of one of the first of the new Lockheed Sirius high-speed sport aircraft, and in it he and Mrs Lindbergh, on 20 April the following year, made a Los Angeles-New York unofficial record flight in 14 hours 23 minutes flying time with only one stop.

This was only the first of a series of pioneering and route-proving flights they undertook together. On 29 July 1931 they took off from College Point, NY, in the Sirius (now Edo float-equipped) on a breathtaking journey to Tokyo—via Canada, Alaska and the tip of Russia.

First stop was North Haven, Me., where Mrs Lindbergh said goodbye to her family. On the next leg, to Ottawa, she had her first successful day

Ann and Charles Lindbergh in their Lockheed Sirius.

The Lindberghs' Lockheed Sirius, in flight now equipped with Edo floats.

with operating the radio, and as the flight progressed she quickly became a highly proficient operator.

The experts at Ottawa were politely concerned at Lindbergh's choice of route. His method was to rule a straight line on the map between the various route stages, regardless of the terrain beneath and independent of recognised embryo air routes. But over featureless swamp and lake the Sirius carried

them, the Cyclone not missing a beat, skirting Hudson Bay via Churchill to the tiny trading outpost at Baker Lake.

During the next leg to Aklavik, Lindbergh took a few cat-naps while his wife took over the controls, and during one of these spells the motor began to splutter. Lindbergh quickly reached for the fuel cocks and the engine again roared into life. But a glance at the vast Mackenzie delta below

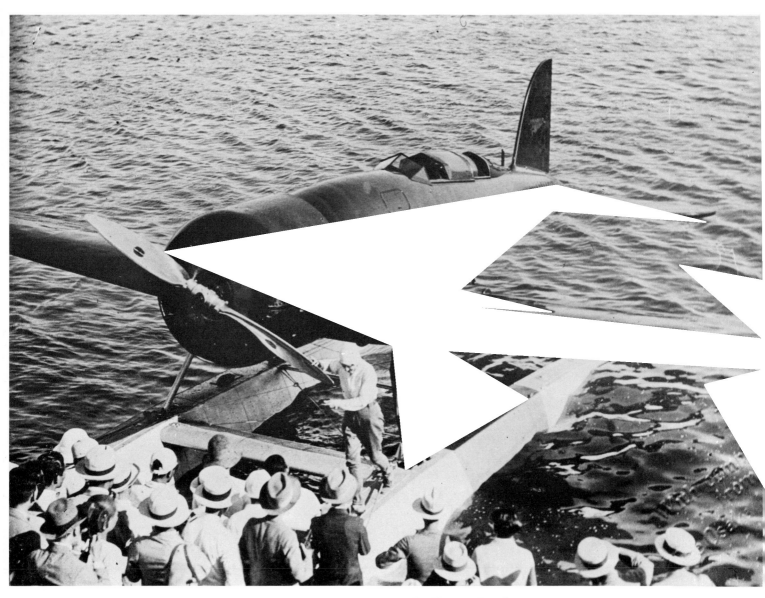

The float-equipped Sirius on one of the later flights.

fully brought home to them the risks of a forced landing so far from civilisation. Grey fog banks, cloud and rain, the weird half-light of an Arctic night accompanied them on this part of the flight.

Further adventures on their journey included a hazardous forced descent in fog and two nights on the open sea in the lee of Ketoi Island, North Japan, and the discovery of an intending stow-away on the plane at Osaka, their next stop after reaching Tokyo. Flying across the Yellow Sea to China, they found the Yangtze River in full spate and volunteered their services to the Flood Relief Commission to survey the flooded areas. And just at the end when their task was almost done, the Sirius was capsised and almost sunk when being hoisted into the Yangtze from the British aircraft carrier *Hermes.*

Saved from the river, the Sirius went to Shanghai on the deck of *Hermes,* and from there was shipped to Lockheed for repair.

The last great journey in the Sirius started on 9 July 1933, when the pair set off on a flight right round the North Atlantic to survey air routes between the U.S.A. and Europe for Pan American. They crossed to Europe via the northern route— Newfoundland, Greenland, Iceland, the Faeroes and Shetlands, to Copenhagen. Then a tour of Europe, including Stockholm, Leningrad, Moscow, Southampton, Galway, Inverness, Amsterdam and Geneva, to Lisbon. Finally an exploration of the middle trans-ocean route as far as the Azores, and a successful crossing of the South Atlantic route from Bathurst, East Africa, to Natal, Brazil. Over five months after they started, having flown nearly 30,000 miles, the Lindberghs arrived back at College Point on 19 December.

Two days later Lindbergh presented the plane, fully equipped, to the American Museum.

The Sirius, altered to Colonel Lindbergh's specification and tested in late 1929 and the spring of 1930, was a Model 8 two-seater landplane version with a Pratt & Whitney 420-hp motor and wood construction, plywood covered. The fuselage was painted black with gold trim lines, and the wings and certain tail surfaces were orange-red. The number 211 used on the famous *Spirit* was retained but with an NR prefix, the registration being carried on the rudder.

With long-range flight plans in mind, Lindbergh ordered extra tankage, mainly in the fuselage, to bring the total fuel load up to 440 gallons for a range of around 3300 miles. The plane, later dubbed 'Tingmissartoq' (in Eskimo 'the one who flies like a big bird') spanned 42 ft 10 in approximately, was 27 ft 6 in long, had a mean chord of 6 ft 10 in, and a wing area of 265 sq ft. Empty weight was 2950 lb and full-range loaded weight 6200 lb compared with a normal loaded weight of 4400 lb. Company figures for average Sirius performance were: top speed 175 mph; cruising speed 145 mph; climb rate 1200 fpm; service ceiling 20,000 ft.

The tone general arrangement drawing shows the plane in slightly cleaned up form with enclosed cockpits, cut-down engine exhausts, and no spinner. For the 1931 flights, floats were added and 300 gallons of fuel stowed therein, enabling a 200-gallon extra fuselage tank to be removed to make more room in the baggage compartment. With the remaining 110-gallon fuselage tank and twin 58-gallon wing tanks, total capacity was up to 526-gallons for the new Cyclone engine fitted, enabling the Colonel always to keep a good fuel reserve in hand on the various legs of the New York-Tokyo flight.

For the 1933 survey flight, a more powerful Wright Cyclone F was installed, giving 710 hp and driving a Hamilton Standard cp propeller.

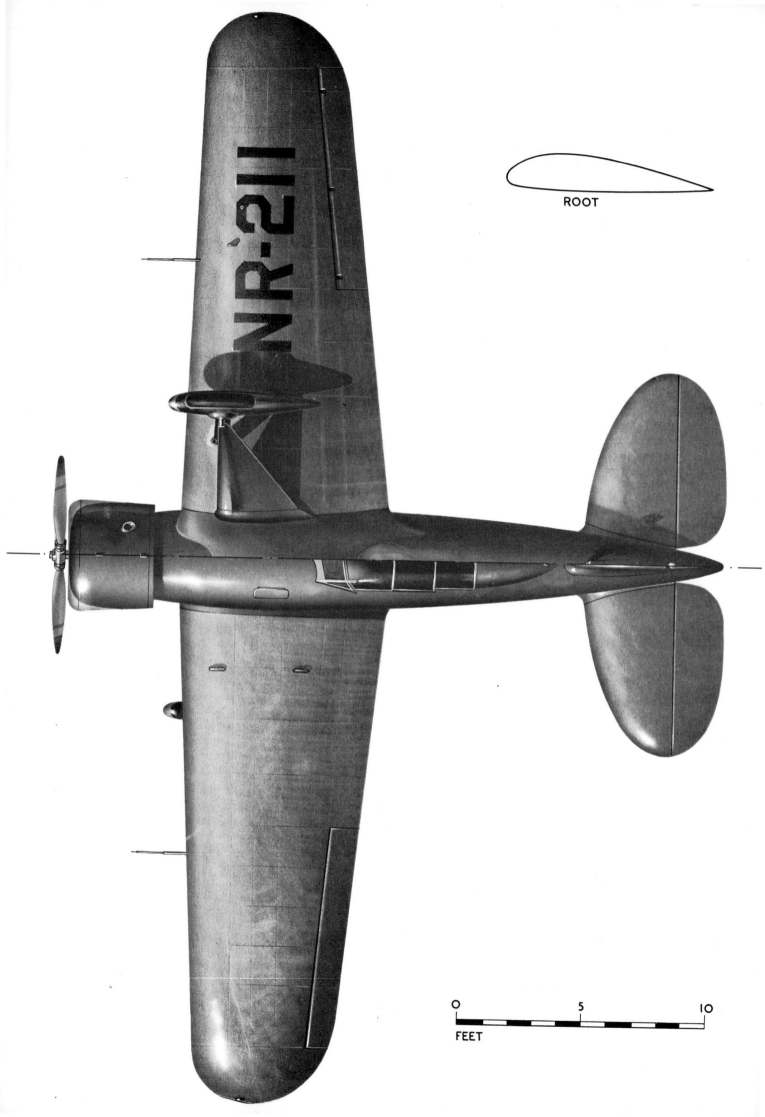

ROOT

0   5   10

FEET

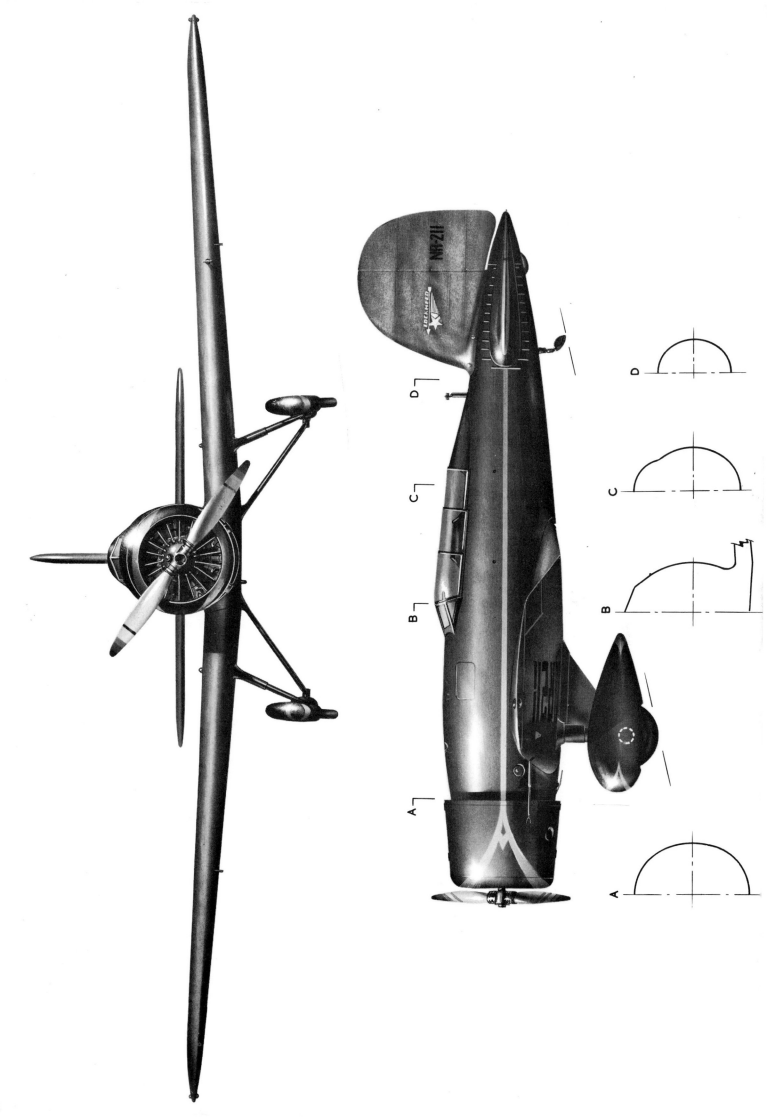

The Schneider Trophy Supermarine S.6B

Flight-Lieutenant John Nelson Boothman, winner of the Schneider Trophy for Britain in 1931.

Flight-Lieutenant G.H. Stainforth on 29 September 1931 created a new Worlds Air Speed record of 407.5 mph in the S6B S1595.

ONE OF AVIATION'S MOST SPECTACULAR series of competitive events was the recurring contest for M. Jacques Schneider's 25,000-franc (in 1912) gold, silver and bronze Trophy offered for an international air race for seaplanes.

The first race was organised by France and took place at Monaco during the Hydro Aeroplane Competitions in April 1913. It was an entirely French affair since the only foreign competitor, C.T. Weymann from the United States, was flying a French twin-float Nieuport. Weymann looked like a winner all the way until a broken oil line forced him down when only three laps from the finish. Provost actually won for France in his Deperdussin monoplane.

Britain had a brilliant victory in the 1914 race at Monaco, when Howard Pixton flew a seaplane version of the speedy Sopwith Tabloid biplane round the 150-sea mile, 28-lap course at an average speed of 86.8 mph.

The First World War caused the next event to be postponed until 1919. England, as holders of the Trophy, were the hosts on this occasion, and the race was flown offshore from Bournemouth over a longer, 220-sea mile, course. Heavy mist turned the race into a fiasco. Janello in the Savoia S13 flying boat gallantly completed the distance but was disqualified because he had not been sighted at one of the markers. No other machine finished the course, so the race was declared null and void, although as some compensation to Janello it was agreed to hold the next contest in Italy.

The 1920 and 1921 events, both in Venice, were scarcely more satisfactory since in both events only Italian machines actually 'raced'. Bologna in a Savioa S19 won the 1920 event at 107.2 mph, and de Briganti was successful the next year in the Macchi M-7 at an average 111 mph. If Italy, with her two consecutive wins, took the 1922 race as well, she would according to the contest rules keep the Trophy for all time.

Naples was the venue for the sixth Schneider contest, in which a three-machine Italian team was opposed by a single British entry, a Sea Lion II biplane flying boat specially prepared at their own expense by Supermarine and Napier. Captain H.C. Biard in the Sea Lion flew a cunning race, to win at an average 145.7 mph, hotly pursued by the Italians.

The Supermarine S6B S1595 which won the Schneider Trophy outright for Britain, piloted by Flight-Lieutenant John Boothman.

Biard and the modified Sea Lion III were among the British challengers for the 1923 race at Cowes, but he, and the French competitor Hurel in a CAMS 38, were outclassed by a strong American challenge from Lieutenants Irvine and Rittenhouse in Navy Curtiss R-3 racers. As distinct from the largely stock designs that hitherto had competed, the Curtiss machines were race-bred from the original 1921 high-speed Pulitzer-winning machine built specially for the US Navy. Henceforth, special racers began to be developed by the other competitors, the speed curve took a steep upward turn and design and engineering advances occurred which gave the later Schneider races their absorbing technical interest.

Rittenhouse won the 1923 race at 177.38 mph, and the following year the United States could have retained the Trophy for a second term, for Italy withdrew her team, and the British entry—the Gloster 2 half-heartedly subsidised by the Air Ministry—sank after landing during its trials at Felixstowe. Very sportingly, and against precedent, the US decided to hold over the race until the following year. As it turned out, she thereby lost her chance to win the Trophy outright, for at Baltimore in 1925 Lieutenant James H. Doolittle beat British, Italian, and US Navy opposition in his Curtiss R3C-2, winning at 232.57 mph. Had the

United States won the 1924 race by a 'fly-over', in 1925 she would have found herself the permanent holder of the Schneider Trophy.

Great Britain could not assemble a team in time for the eighth race in 1926, but formidable opposition came at the last moment from a full Italian team flying sleek new Macchi M-39 monoplanes powered by 800-hp Fiat engines. The R3C-2 was again in the U.S. team together with the other 1925 machines, re-engined as the R3C-2 and R3C-4. Lieutenant Cuddihy's R3C-4 closely tailed de Bernardi in the M-39 until forced down with fuel pump failure, the Italian won in convincing style at 246.496 mph. The Trophy went back to Italy, and it was still anyone's contest.

Great Britain girded her loins in readiness for the 1927 event in Venice. For the first time full Air Ministry support was given, with proper service personnel and special machines. No less than seven racers were ordered from British manufacturers. Those which went to Venice were three Supermarine S.5s and two Gloster 4s, all Napier Lion-powered, and the Short Crusader with an aircooled Bristol Mercury engine. The Italian team was strong, too, with the hush-hush new Macchi M-52s.

During the race all the Italian entrants and Kinkead's 289-mph Gloster 4 dropped out with

R.A. Mitchell's first racing monoplane seaplane, the S4, was in advance of its time and not a success, but led to the famous S5 and S6 series seaplanes which eventually won the Schneider Trophy outright for Britain.

various mechanical troubles, leaving the two S.5s to complete the course. Webster in the geared S.5 was the winner at 281.656 mph, with Worsley second in the ungeared machine at 272.96 mph.

It having been agreed to hold the race every two years thereafter, the next event—at Ryde, Isle of Wight—was in 1929. This event saw the mating of the genius of R.J. Mitchell, designer of the Supermarine racers, and the Rolls-Royce engine team. Mitchell evolved from his earlier Schneider designs the beautiful S.6, powered by a special race engine based on the 825-hp Rolls-Royce Buzzard, giving a bit under 1950 hp at 3000 rpm. Gloster entered with a formidable team-mate, the Gloster 6 monoplane with a racing Napier Lion VIID giving around 1200 hp, which did not eventually compete due to fuel system faults.

The Italians requested—but were refused—extra time to perfect their latest machines, but nevertheless put in a strong team headed by the new 350-mph, 1400-hp Macchi M-67s. The United States entry, Lieutenant Al Williams in a Mercury midwing monoplane, was refused navy permission to race—the second time he had tried and failed to compete in the Schneider event.

The race started on 7 September at 2 p.m., Waghorn getting away smartly in his S.6, followed by Dal Molin's Macchi M-52 and then in succession by the S.5, a Macchi M-67, the second S.6, and the other M-67. Molin flew a fine steady race to second place in the veteran M-52, but both the M-67s dropped out early, Cadringher's when he was blinded and nearly suffocated by exhaust fumes, and Monti's with a broken water pipe which caused him some bad scalds. Waghorn flew a consistent race in the S.6 number 2 to win at 328.63 mph,

with Acherley bidding for second place at 325.54 mph despite difficulty in keeping on course due to the loss of his goggles—in fact, he was later disqualified for cutting inside one of the markers.

Three days later Squadron Leader Orlebar took up the Schneider-winning S.6 and set a new world's speed record of 355.8 mph.

For two events in succession, therefore, full Government support—in the form of adequate funds and the formation of the High Speed Flight—had brought home the Trophy to Britain. With the better part of two years to prepare for the 1931 race, and with a faultless performance from the 1929 machines and engines as a basis for an even better technical effort, Britain had a good chance of winning the Trophy outright. Month after month went by, however, without an official announcement as to the Air Ministry's 1931 Schneider plans. A nation-wide outcry followed the eventual long-delayed decision by an economy-minded Labour Government that official support was to be withdrawn and that any further entry would have to be left to private enterprise. Bearing in mind the prohibitive cost even of modifying the existing machines, this seemed to mean that Britain would be unable to provide machines for the next contest, although a nucleus of the High Speed Flight personnel remained in being for experimental work.

The ruin of Britain's hopes of keeping the Schneider Trophy was brought to the attention of Lucy Houston, the richest woman in England. In 1933 Lady Houston financed the British Houston Flight over Mount Everest, but the deed for which British aviation is most indebted to her was her response to this present crisis.

Evolved from the S4, the Napier-engined S5 won the 1927 Schneider Trophy race for Britain.

Something appropaching £100,000 was needed, and she straightaway wrote a cheque which put new life and hope into the Supermarine and Rolls-Royce design office staffs. As only a few months remained before the event, there was no time to evolve a completely new design. Instead, the S.6 combination had to be developed to a point where it would stand a chance against scheduled French and Italian opposition.

Rolls-Royce had promised an extra 400 hp or so from the 1929 engine, and the Air Ministry therefore ordered Supermarine to build two new improved machines, S.6s, for the main race effort, and modify the two 1929 S.6s as S.6As as a second string.

Beginning work on the engine, Rolls decided to increase the engine speed and supercharger gear ratio, and enlarge the air intake. A new type of connecting rod and a modified crankcase and balanced crankshaft were fitted. In an effort to bring down fuel consumption (because of new contest regulations requiring two succeeding take-offs and thus extra fuel), sodium-filled exhaust valves as developed in the United States were successfully used to allow a leaner mixture. Carburettors had to be redesigned to prevent flooding in flat turns, and fuel ingredients carefully blended to balance power and consumption. In the end, practically the whole engine was redesigned, so close had been the design limits of the 1929 models.

All this added up to frantic test work on the engines during the short months preceding the race. By the end of April 1931, engine life on the bench was only an average 20 minutes before some kind of failure. By the end of July, 30 minutes was the mean. On 3 August a 58-minute run was accomplished at 2360 bhp, and about a month before the race, on 12 August, a full hour's trouble-free run was completed at 2330 bhp.

The S.6 series racers were basically fairly conventional all-metal structures, although the monocoque fuselage featured very close spacing (about six to seven inches) of some 46 light frames, and the motor bearers were extended rearwards almost to the tail to form the main longitudinal members. Behind the large engine bay was a sloping bulkhead with fireproof, metal-asbestos sandwich lower half which kept a good deal of heat away from the pilot. Wings were of two-spar metal construction with 9½-inch rib spacing.

Main design problem with the S.6, as with other contemporary Schneider designs, had been the adequate dissipation of the enormous heat output from the racing engine. Honeycomb radiators thrust out into the airstream would have provided the best solution to the difficulty but ruined the streamlining. Instead, practically the whole wing covering was made in the form of thin double-skin radiators with 1/16-inch between-walls water passages, screwed as units to the wing structure. Later, as cooling was still inadequate, louvres were cut in the underside of the wing to direct cooling air on the insides of the radiators.

Main oil coolers were in the form of exterior corrugations on the sides and belly of the fuselage extending practically its whole length. The fin and part of the rear decking formed the integral oil

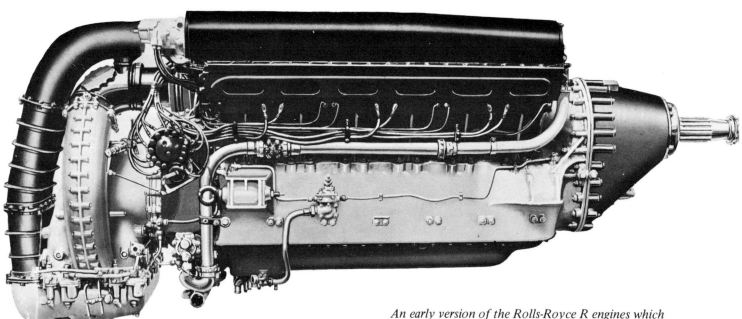

An early version of the Rolls-Royce R engines which powered the later Supermarine racing seaplanes.

tank, which therefore obtained some additional cooling from the slipstream.

As mentioned already, for 1931 the sea-worthiness trials were to be done immediately before the start, involving a take-off at full load, a landing, a brief taxi, and then another take-off for the race proper. So extra fuel had to be provided to leave enough for the whole seven-lap event. All-up weight was 19 per cent greater than in 1929, which meant that extra buoyancy was needed from the floats. Redesign of the floats thus became of paramount importance, and following extensive water-tank and wind-tunnel tests a design markedly superior to that used in 1929 was evolved. Variations of the new float design were fitted to all four machines, those on the S.6As being two inches shorter than the S.6Bs. The main 110-gallon fuel tank was built into the starboard float to offset the weight transfer (estimated at 500 lb) caused by engine torque. Total fuel capacity was 161½ gallons, of which 48 were in the other float and 3½ in a header tank.

The 1929 S.6 carried small water coolers on the sides of the floats—since practically every inch of wing and fuselage surface were occupied by oil or water radiators—and still cooling was scarcely adequate. For the 1931 machines the whole float decking was made a radiator in the same manner as the wing covering. No wonder these planes were sometimes dubbed 'flying radiators'.

Propeller design created difficulties, the aim being to give more take-off thrust as well as converting the extra power into thrust at an estimated 365-mph top speed. A smaller-diameter airscrew was favoured, but on its first test the machine swung so badly in fast taxying that a take-off could not be attempted. Eventually a 1929 propeller cut down to 9 ft 1½ in diameter was used for the Schneider fly-round and a

strengthened 9 ft 6 in airscrew for the speed record attempts.

In May 1931 the High Speed Flight moved to Calshot for advanced training. Team commander was Squadron Leader Orlebar and the members Flight-Lieutenants Hope, Long, Boothman, and Stainforth, Lieutenant Brinton (killed in the S.6A N247 during training), and Flying Officer Snaith. Initial training was done on two S.5s, two Gloster 6s and a Gloster 4, but later the two S.6As (N247 and N248) were received, followed in July by the S.6Bs, S1595 and S1596. The S.6As initially used the 1929-type engines, but later N248, at least, was re-engined with the boosted 1931 motor.

A win in the contest depended not only on the technical superiority of the planes. The high standard of flying achieved by the High Speed Flight was reached after prolonged and scientific investigation of the flying problems posed by the triangular 1931 course. For example, it was found that the least time was lost at the markers by keeping the turns wide and steady and the loading limited to around 3g. To ease the effects of g loads on the pilots in turns, and prevent the consequent 'blacking out', oxygen was tried as a stimulant, but with no success. Another suggested solution was the adoption of an abdominal belt inflated from an airstream intake—an early application of the g-suit idea.

Abroad, meanwhile, the French and Italian opposition were having their troubles, too. Pilots in both countries were killed. The Italians had a new Macchi said to use two 12-cylinder Fiat motors set end to end, the whole 24-cylinder unit driving contra-props. This machine later became well-known as the speed-record Macchi MC-72, but it was too advanced to be ready in time for the 1931 race and the Italians had to retire. French plans never came to much, so Great Britain was left as

Companion to the Trophy-winning S1595, the S6B S1596 flown by Stainforth set a new temporary World's Air Speed record of 379.05 mph on 13 September 1931, only to be beaten by her sister ship with the same pilot later that month.

the sole competitor.

The last Schneider event, on 13 September 1931, was thus something of an anticlimax as a spectacle. Britain entered the two S.6Bs and the remaining S.6A. Boothman drew the straw for the first attempt and took off in S1595 (race number 1). He made his first landing after the prescribed brief hop, did his two minutes or so taxying, and then roared away again for the actual fly-round. He flew an easy seven laps, nursing a heating engine on the water guage and going well wide in the turns, to finish the course at an average 340.8 mph and win the Trophy outright for Britain. At 4 p.m. on the same afternoon Stainforth took up S1596, which had been standing by in case Boothman failed, to try for the world speed record. Of five runs made over the 3-kilometre course, the last four averaged out a new record of 379.05 mph. The engine used was the R25 giving 2340 hp at 3200 maximum revs.

Rolls had up their sleeve a special sprint engine, number R27, which with some internal strengthening and using methanol, acetone, benzol and T.E.L. gave 2530 hp at 3200 maximum revs—for a short period. At 6 p.m. on 29 September in failing light Stainforth took up S1595, now fitted with the sprint engine and with 100 gallons of fuel on board, for another try at the record. On his first run he achieved 415.2 mph, and the average of the last four of five runs worked out at 407.5 mph.

The S.6B serial S1595, outright winner of the Schneider Trophy, and world speed record holder, is featured in the tone fourview drawing. Wings, tailplane, struts, float tops, wire bracing, fuselage flash and parts of the engine top cowling are aluminium; the propeller is aluminium with black-painted backs to the blades and polished spinner; the rest of the machine is dark blue. The race number '1' is in white on the fuselage sides; the

sighting line on the port wing is blue; serial numbers on the tail are black, outlined in white on the red and blue stripes.

This machine is permanently on show in the National Aeronautical Collection, Science Museum, London. Data are as follows (with that for the S.6A, where different, in brackets): overall length 28 ft 10 in (28 ft 8 in); float track 7 ft 6 in; wing span 30 ft; wing chord 5 ft 8 in; loaded weight 6070 lb for race and 5751 lb for second record attempt (heaviest weight at which N248 flew was 5717 lb); wing area 145 sq ft; wing section RAF27; typical wing loading 42 lb/sq ft (39.8 lb/sq ft).

Air Chief Marshal Sir John Boothman died in London in December 1957 aged 56. After the 1931 Schneider event he did experimental work at Martlesham Heath test establishment, went on to Staff duties, visited Washington during the war as advisor to the USAAF on RAF bombing techniques and held operational posts. After the war he had a spell as AOC-in-C, RAF Coastal Command, and a top appointment in NATO before retiring in 1956. Apart from many British and foreign decorations, he held the American DFC and was a Commander of the Legion of Merit (USA).

Stainforth, a Wing Commander and crack night-fighter pilot—said to be the oldest fighter pilot in the Middle East—was killed in action there in 1942.

Mitchell, Supermarine's designer, and Rolls-Royce undoubtedly learned a lot from the Schneider Trophy machines, experience which stood them in good stead when they came to design the Spitfire and the Merlin. That experience alone was worth every penny of Lady Houston's £100,000 and the other money, private and public, which went into the S.6 series.

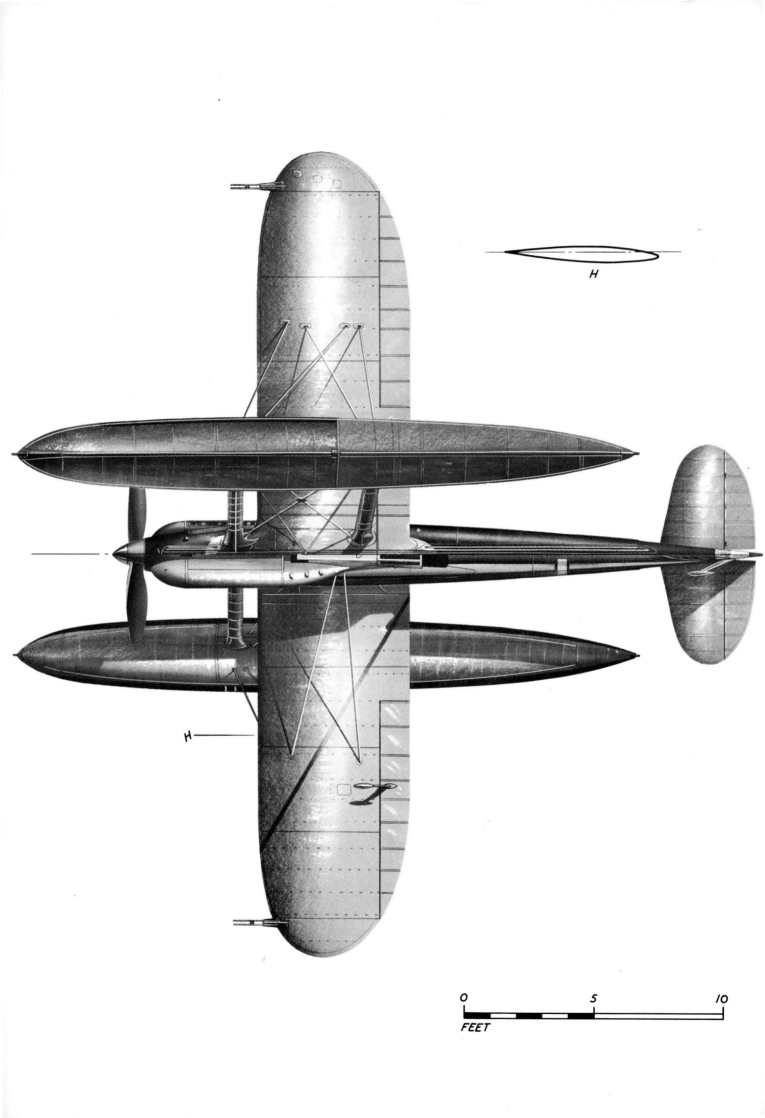

H

H

0   5   10

FEET

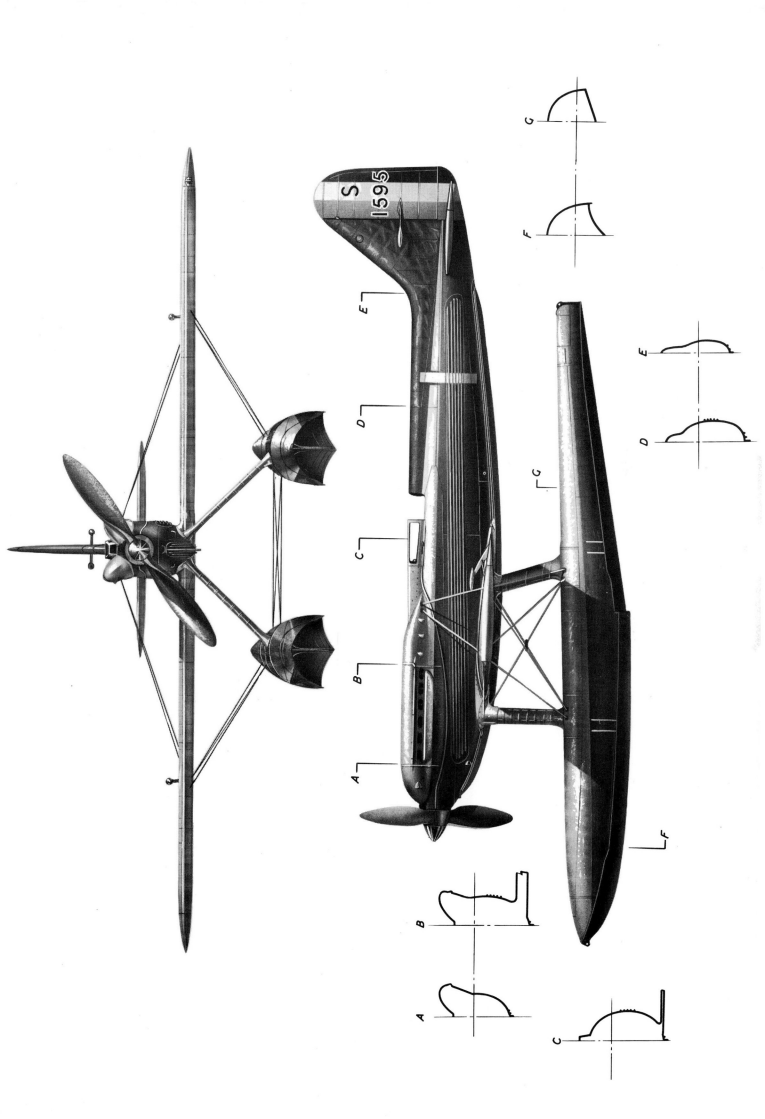

Jimmy Doolittle's Gee Bee

Doolittle in front of an air force fighter.

OF THE NINE speedsters lined up for Event 15, the Charles Thompson Trophy race, at the 1932 National Air Races at Cleveland, the two Gee Bee racers most intrigued the massed crowd of spectators. A bewildering variety of design features was to be expected from the many manufacturers, design groups and syndicates which each year entered their hottest racing planes in the three-year-old free-for-all Thompson event.

But the barrel-shaped R-1 and R-2 struck a different note even among the miscellany of the National Air Races. The NACA-type cowling on each swelled out aft of the cylinder heads instead of closely enveloping the motor, its lines being continued by a bulbous fuselage which merged imperceptibly into the vestige of a tail. The cockpit was a tiny excrescence fairing directly into the fin, seeming scarcely large enough for a man to squeeze through. In fact entry into the cockpit was usually made through a door in the starboard side of the fuselage, although the hood could be released in an emergency.

There was some down-to-earth design thinking behind this unorthodox streamlined shape, ideas already tested in the wind tunnel with scale models in a new effort to overcome the severe frontal area drag of the radial engine. Given this blunt entry, it was determined that the best streamlined shape should have its maximum thickness about a third of the way back from the nose—a true teardrop shape in fact. In following this design criterion, Granville Brothers Aircraft Inc., who built the planes, decided to ignore convention and created the stubby fuselage shape, with enormous cross-sectional area compared to its length, which long since has claimed its place in the history of aeronautical design.

The R-1's pilot on this occasion has carved an even greater niche for himself in aviation history. James Harold Doolittle's first exploit to become nation-wide news was a coast-to-coast flight from Pablo Beach, Fla., to San Diego, Calif., with but one stop, the first time the continent had been spanned in less than 24 hours. The plane was a modified DH-4, the dates were 4 and 5 September 1922, the time 22 hours 34 minutes and the average speed 101 mph.

A piloting genius who quickly came to recognise the value of an academic background to his

This view of the Gee Bee R-1 well illustrates the bulbous shape and colourful paint scheme. In this view the wire bracing, tiny faired cockpit cover and controllable-pitch airscrew are clearly seen.

practical air experiments, Doolittle got his Master of Science degree at the Massachusetts Institute of Technology in 1924, and his Doctor of Science degree in Aeronautical Engineering the following year.

In the meantime he did vital flight research on service machines, systematically probing the structural limitations of current fighter planes during violent manoeuvres and the effects of g forces on the pilot. Ice-cold courage, superb airmanship and a background of technical know-how were distilled into NACA Report No 203 enumerating his findings during these tests, a report which fundamentally affected the specifications for new warplanes then being drawn up by the Army Air Corps.

This vital work on aircraft accelerations was carried out far from the public gaze, but his next exploit again hit the headlines. Piloting the Curtiss R3C-2 seaplane, which in landplane form flown by Lieutenant Cyrus Bettis had won the 1925 Pulitzer Trophy race, Doolittle won the 1925 Schneider Trophy race against navy, British and Italian opposition at 232.573 mph, and then topped this with a 245.713-mph world's record for seaplanes.

Yet another brilliant piece of flying was his work under the auspices of the Daniel Guggenheim Fund on the development of blind flying aids—including the Sperry artifical horizon and directional gyro, and the sensitive Kollsman barometric altimeter—which culminated with the first under-the-hood take-off, flight and landing, started in fog and accomplished with the sole aid of the cockpit instruments.

Resigning his army commission in February 1930, Jimmy Doolittle went into the oil business with Shell, helping sales along with many appearances as a demonstration and racing pilot. He won the first Bendix Trophy race in 1931 with his new Laird Super-Solution, taking off again for New York after the official finish at Cleveland to create a new coast-to-coast record in 11 hours 16 minutes 10 seconds.

The following year he again intended to enter his now modified Laird in the Bendix race, and sent it to be fitted with a new retracting landing gear in an effort to raise the high cruising speed. The plane was wrecked, however, when he belly-landed after the undercarriage had refused to wind down for the landing. From the many offers of a

Jimmy Doolittle poses in front of the Gee Bee racer R-1.

manoeuvrability than the slower contestants, Doolittle flew the R-1 in shallow-banked wide-radius curves about the pylons in an effort to keep up the speed in the turns, and it soon became evident that the ten-lap race was a forgone conclusion in his favour barring error or mechanical trouble. He romped home an easy winner at an average 252.686 mph. The R-1 had already gained a new landplane speed record of 296.287 mph on 3 September.

Fastest landplane of its day, the R-1 had numerous interesting technical features. The motor was a 750/800 hp Pratt & Whitney Wasp Sr displacing 1344 cc. Compression ratio was 6:1 and the supercharger ratio 12:1. The Smith metal c.p. propeller had settings from 20-28 degrees controlled in flight from the cockpit, and during the race was set at its maximum travel almost as soon as the machine was airborne.

The fuselage had a fineness ratio of roughly 3.5:1 and was basically a chrome-molybdenum steel diagonally-braced tubular structure with welded joints, faired to a circular section at the front portion and tapering back to a vertical knife edge at the rudder. The top of the fin was offset to port to counteract engine torque, and the horizontal stabiliser was adjustable over 15 degrees. Handholes were provided on each side of the cockpit decking to enable the pilot to wipe over the outside of the shatterproof glass windscreen in flight.

new plane for the air races, he accepted one from the Granvilles to fly the powerful Gee Bee R-1.

Gently but firmly, Doolittle handled this mettlesome plane as he had all the others. For the Thompson race, the Gee Bees were fitted with Smith controllable-pitch airscrews, and the R-1 fairly leaped off the ground to take the lead almost immediately. With plenty of brute power but less

Wing stubs were integral with the fuselage structure, with wooden outer panels built up around two solid spruce spars reinforced with duralumin plates. Spruce and plywood ribs spaced five inches apart were covered with Haskelite plywood and then doped fabric.

Wheel spats moved with the wheels on their five-inch compression and rebound travel. Aircraft Products wheelbrakes were applied by pulling the stick hard back, or with a differential action from the rudder pedals.

The R-2 flown into fifth place in the Thompson Trophy race by Lee Gehlbach was basically the same as Doolittle's mount but was designed from the start for the Bendix cross-country event and had less power (a 550-hp Wasp Jr) and extra tankage.

The tone GA drawing shows the R-1 in flying attitude, with the landing gear shock struts uncompressed. The colourful paint scheme was in red and white with a thin black line dividing the colours. Lettering, dice and numerals were red on white or white on red, with the large racing number 11 and the registration outlined with a black line and applied on the wing parallel to the line of flight. 'WASP' was painted on the cowling, as were the numbers '7' and '11' separated by four dice with 'speed lines' and the initials S.A.R.A. for the Springfield Air Racing Association. 'Gee Bee Super Sportster' was in script on the fuselage aft of the canopy. Other inscriptions were 'Goodrich Tires' and 'Aircraft Products Co. Brakes and Wheels' on the spats; 'Engine Cowl and Boots by Hill Aircraft Streamliners' on the leg fairings; and 'Manufactured by—Granville Bros. Aircraft Inc. Springfield Airport, Springfield, Mass.' and 'Titanine Finish' on the rudder.

Data on the plane are: span 25 ft; length 17 ft 9 in; chord near wing root 4 ft 5 in; wing incidence 2.5 degrees; wing dihedral 4.5 degrees; wheel track 6 ft 4 in; empty weight 1840 lb; gross weight with full tanks 3075 lb; normal loaded weight with 50 gallons fuel 2415 lb; fuel tankage 160 gallons; oil tankage 18 gallons.

Not long after his triumph in the 1932 Thompson Trophy race, Jimmy Doolittle announced his retirement from the more spectacular types of piloting to devote himself to the oil business. Fate must have smiled, for his greatest piloting and organisational triumph was years in the future.

Back on active duty in June 1940 he first had various staff jobs and then a spell at AAF Headquarters in Washington, DC. Then out of the blue he was picked by General Henry H. Arnold for an incredible mission, the bombing of Japan by army bombers taking off from an aircraft carrier.

The famed 'Doolittle Raid' took place on 18 April 1942. Sixteen B-25 medium bombers crewed by 79 volunteers and led personally by Doolittle, then a Lieutenant-Colonel, took off from the carrier *Hornet* 800 miles out from the enemy shore, en route for Tokyo, Kobe, Nogoya, Yokohama, Kenagwa and Yokesuike to crash the first American bombs on the Japanese mainland.

In 1946, after a brilliant wartime record, Brigadier-General Doolittle reverted to inactive Reserve status and returned to Shell. Later he was chairman of NACA, for which body in earlier years he did so much flying research, and of the Air Force Scientific Advisory Board. Today, as a young 74-year-old, he still plays an active part in business and with government, philanthropic and educational organisations and committees.

Presentation of Congressional Medal of Honor to Brigadier General James H. Doolittle by President Roosevelt 20 May, 1942. Left to Right: *President Roosevelt, Lt. General Henry H. Arnold, Mrs Doolittle, Brigadier General James H. Doolittle and General George C. Marshall, Chief of Staff.*

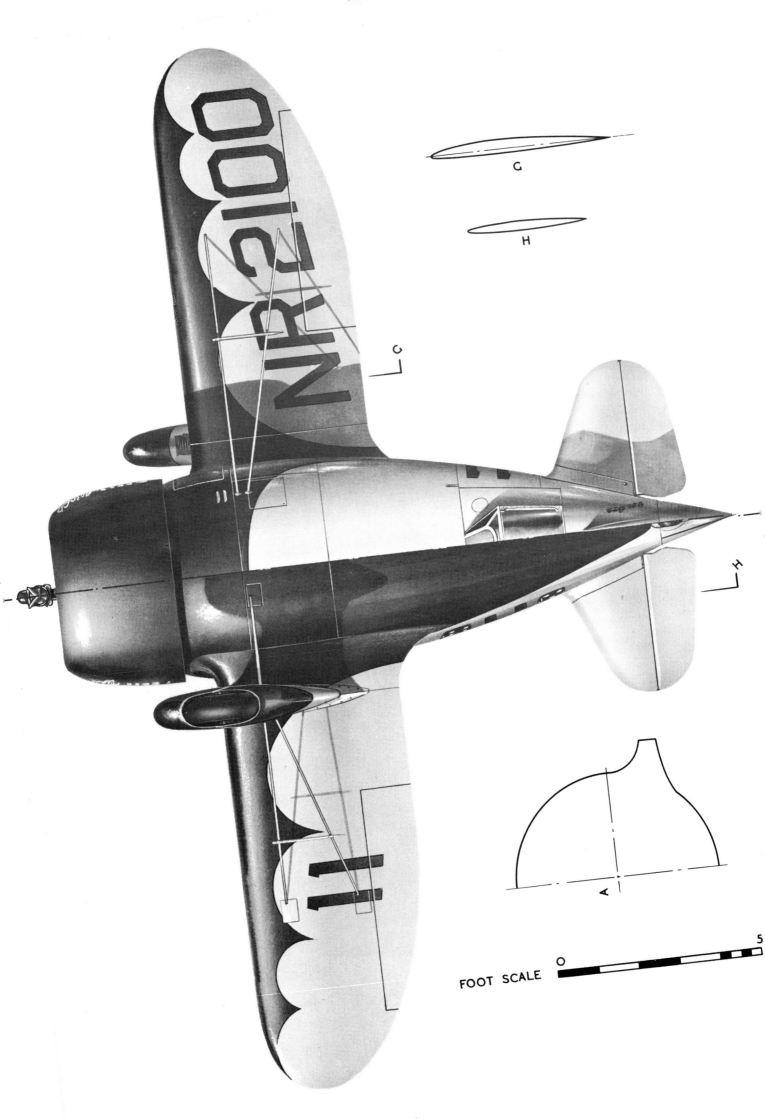

G

H

C

H

A

FOOT SCALE

0 5

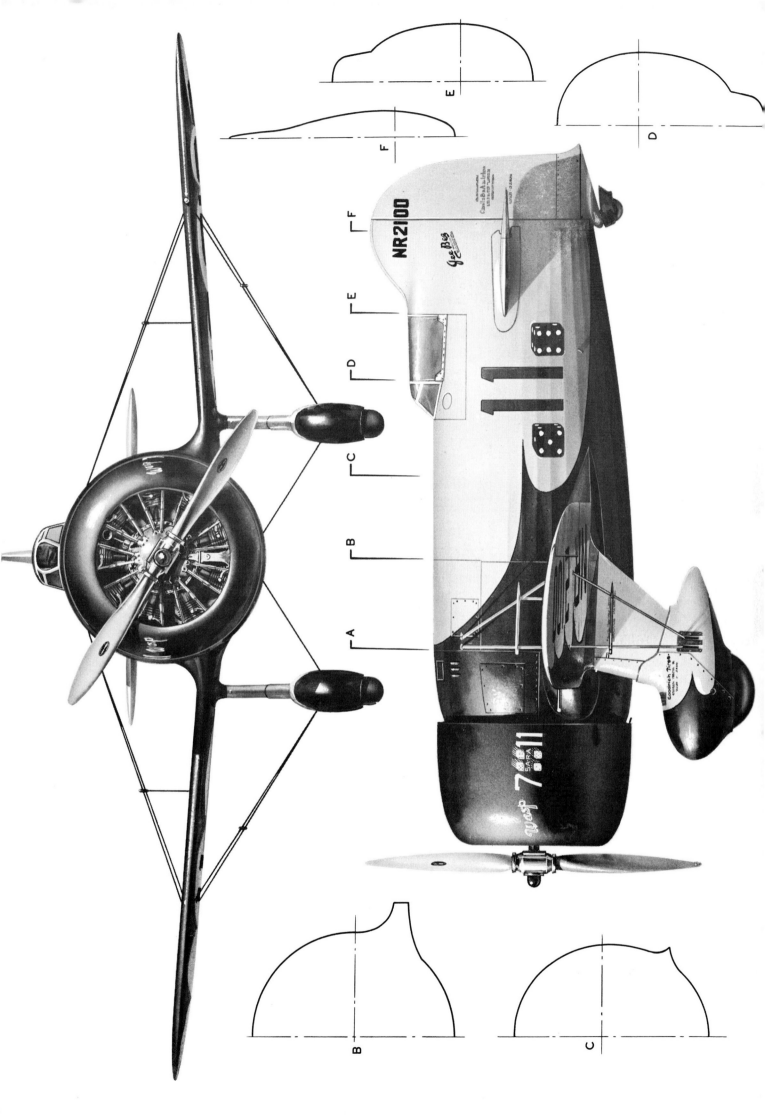

Charles Scott and Tom Campbell Black in the cockpit of the de Havilland Comet.

DESIGN-FOR-A-PURPOSE personified—that was the original DH88 Comet. No extraneous considerations were allowed to mar the machine's ideal conception as a long-distance high-speed racer. The fuselage was a beautifully streamlined fuel and crew container, the big fuel tanks being carried over the wing near to the center of gravity, relegating the crew to a position farther aft than was strictly best from the visibility standpoint. Engines were comparatively low in power to keep down fuel consumption—two were needed to give the speed and reliability/safety factor.

The wing was thin, the landing gear retractable, two-position airscrews were fitted and so were flaps. Every modern device was used, in fact, to get at least 220 mph at low consumption over a 2500-mile-plus range.

Sole purpose of the design was to win the MacRobertson England-Australia Trophy race of 1934. Sir William MacPherson Robertson was an Australian tycoon in the confectionery business, and a citizen of Melbourne. He offered £15,000 total prize money plus organising expenses for an

The Comet under preparation for the race.

air race between England and Melbourne, Victoria, as part of the centenary celebrations of that State. The race was to be in two sections, speed and handicap, with the winners getting £10,000 and a gold trophy, and £2000, respecitvely.

As entries began to come in, it became obvious that the race would probably be a walkover for one of the American planes entered. Partly due to geographical and economic conditions in the U.S.A., that country could show several suitable long-range high-speed aeroplanes. Using high-power radials developed to a fine pitch, and also advanced mechanical features—variable-pitch airscrews, flaps, retractable landing gears—sometimes invented abroad but allowed to languish in their country of origin, such planes as the Douglas DC-2 and Boeing 247D were well ahead of their foreign contemporaries. It looked as though English competitors would be relegated to the position of 'also-rans'.

De Havilland, by then well established at Hatfield as makers of sporting and transport aeroplanes, decided to challenge the threatened U.S.

supremacy in the race, and announced in the aeronautical press their offer to build a special racer for the event, guaranteeing over 200 mph top speed, provided orders were placed within a deadline terminating on the last day of February 1934. This would leave them a minimum of less then eight months to design, build and fly the racer. The price quoted was £5000.

First to take the offer were the famed fliers Jim and Amy Mollison, followed by racing motorist Bernard Rubin, and then Mr A.O. Edwards, head of London's Grosvenor House Hotel.

De Havilland used every scrap of modern aeronautical knowledge and the latest mechanical features in their classic twin-engine layout, later to be repeated with the same success in their wartime Mosquito. Light weight and low drag were the keynotes of the all-wood construction. Special versions of the de Havilland Gipsy Six inverted, six-cylinder, aircooled, in-line engines were developed with increased compression and rpm,

The Comet clean, polished and in racing trim.

giving 224 hp at 2400 rpm at sea level and driving French Ratier two-position automatic airscrews. Main fuel was carried in two tanks (128 and 110 gallons) in front of the cockpit, behind which was a further 20-gallon tank for trimming, in all giving a full-throttle range of 2580 miles at 10,000 ft and rather more at cruise setting. Maximum speed was around 235 mph at sea level; cruising speed at 10,000 ft 220 mph; best initial rate of climb 1200 ft min in fine pitch; absolute ceiling (coarse pitch) 19,000 ft; stall with flaps down 78 mph. Weights were: empty 3003 lb; loaded 5550 lb. Wing loading was 26.1 lb/sq in; span 44 ft; length 29 ft 1 in; height 9 ft; wing area 212.5 sq ft.

Mr A.O. Edwards' Comet was ready just eight days before the race and was to be flown by Charles W.A. Scott and Tom Campbell Black. Scott had already made an Australia-and-back solo flight in 1931 and another solo to Australia in 1932 in DH Gipsy Moths, and Black too was an experienced long-distance flier. Their machine, registered G-ACSS and painted signal red, is featured in the tone general arrangement drawing. The name *Grosvenor House* painted on each side of the nose, the fuselage flash, and the registration letters on the fuselage sides and above and below the wing, were white. The race number 34 was painted black on an oval silver ground on the rudder. Spinners and airscrews were natural metal finish.

The Comet's chief competitors in the race were the KLM DC-2 flown by Parmentier and Moll, which eventually came second to the winning Comet and first in the handicap section; Jackie Cochran and Wesley Smith in the Gee Bee *Q.E.D.* (they retired from the race in Roumania); and the Boeing 247D piloted by Colonel Roscoe Turner and Clyde Pangborn, who came third in the speed section.

Scott and Black got away from Mildenhall, Suffolk, on 20 October 1934 after the Mollisons, who in their black and gold *Black Magic* (Comet G-ACSP) were well in the lead on their first 2330-mile hop to Baghdad but later had to withdraw at Allahabad with engine trouble. The third Comet, the Rubin-owned green and white G-ACSR flown by Cathcart Jones and Ken Waller, reached Melbourne only after four and a half hair-raising days, but the crew turned right round again and flew her back to England to create a record for the round trip of 13 days 6 hours.

Scott and Black drove into bad visibility over the Continent which persisted until they were approaching Turkey. After an emergency landing at Kirkuk they slipped into Baghdad just in time to see the Mollisons take off, but on the leg to Allahabad they passed *Black Magic* and landed first. On the 2210-mile stage to Singapore their lead increased, despite battling through storms for the latter part. By now they were very tired as they

The Mollisons preparing to take off in their Comet Black Magic.

took off once more and headed out over Borneo and the Timor Sea, graveyard of many planes and pilots. To fatigue was added apprehension as the oil gauge for the port engine began to lose pressure. They reached Darwin on the mainland of Australia with only one engine, tried unsuccessfully to find the engine fault, and, heart in mouth, took off for Charleville inland with full load and pulling maximum power on the failing engine. They never did find a fault in that engine, for the trouble later turned out to be due to the oil gauge itself, but all the way to Melbourne they had to nurse the power. They landed in Melbourne in pouring rain at 3.30 p.m. on 23 October, more dead than alive. Scott's comment after reviving slightly was: 'It was a lousy trip and that's praising it.'

But they had won the 11,700-mile event in 70 hours 54 minutes 18 seconds, including six intermediate landings, at an average flying speed of 176.8 mph.

Grosvenor House was later bought by the Air Ministry for testing and numbered K5084. Back on the civilian register, in 1937 it was piloted by Ken Waller in the King's Cup race, by A.E. Clouston in the Istre-Damascus race, and from Croydon to Cape Town and back by Clouston and Mrs Kirby Green. In March 1938 it achieved another notable flight of over 26,000 miles to New Zealand and back crewed by Clouston and Victor Ricketts, breaking 11 records on the way.

It spent the war under a tarpaulin on a British airfield but was rescued and eventually rebuilt by students of the de Havilland Technical School at Chester. It now forms part of the Shuttleworth Collection housed at Old Warden aerodrome, Bedfordshire.

In 1935 two other Comets were built: F-ANPZ for the French Government, and G-ADEF for a record attempt to Cape Town by Campbell Black and G. C. McArthur. The latter machine was destroyed after Black and McArthur baled out near Khartoum because of propeller trouble.

F

G-ACSS

FEET
0   5   10

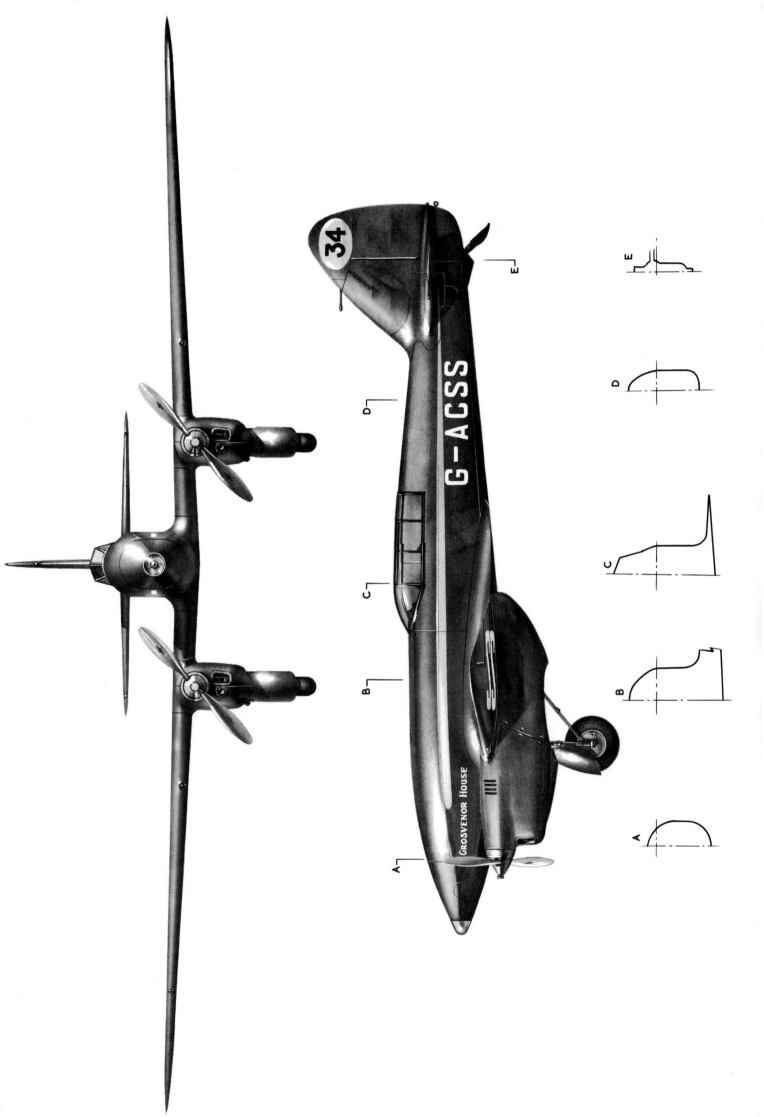

Hero of the Soviet Union Valeri Chkalov, commander of the June 1937 Moscow to Vancouver (Washington) flight.

BIGGEST-SPANNED and heaviest of several special long-range record monoplanes built by various countries in the late 'twenties and 'thirties was the Russian ANT-25.

Conceived in 1932, when Russel Boardman and John Polando held the 5011.8-mile New York-Constantinople record in their Bellanca *Cape Cod*, the ANT-25 did not finally achieve success until 1937, but in the meantime several interesting flights were undertaken.

In September 1934, as an initial test of the plane, the famous Russian flier Gromov with crew members Filin and Spirin made a closed-circuit flight reported at 5700 miles, but failed to beat the existing record.

Levanevsky, in a 1935 Moscow-San Francisco attempt, had to land in Siberia with an oil leak after a 3730-mile flight.

Then, in July 1936, Valeri Chkalov, Alexander Beliakov and George Biadukov made a long-distance flight over the unexplored regions of the Soviet Arctic along what was termed the Stalin Route. Stalin took a great interest in the development of the ANT-25. He saw in it a symbol of prestige for the growing Soviet aircraft industry, and as a propaganda weapon—should it be successful—of the 'peaceful' Communist expansionist doctrine.

The 1936 flight was non-stop from Moscow to the mouth of the Amur River, near Nikolayevsk—via Franz Josef Land, Sevenaya, Zemlya, Yakutia, Petropavlovsk, Sea of Okhotsk. Owing to bad weather, a landing was made on the Island of Udd, one of what were later called the Chkalov Islands also in honour of the plane's commander. The distance flown was just over 5800 miles. A map of the route was later painted on the tail of the ANT-25.

Chkalov and Biadukov were military test pilots, and Beliakov a crack navigation expert and instructor for the Red Air Force. After the 1936 flight, they all returned to regular duty, their appetites whetted for another try the following season. Meantime, trips were made to TSAGI in Moscow where development work on the plane and test flying proceeded, in co-operation with the engineering staff headed by Comrades Stoman and Berdnik.

The fliers had as their goal an extension of the

Stalin converses with Chkalov at the Moscow aerodrome prior to the start of the flight on June 18th 1937.

Stalin route right over the North Pole to North America. The idea had previously been vetoed by Stalin in favour of the less ambitious Moscow-Chkalov Islands journey to test the plane and crew. With the experience of that flight behind him Chkalov again put forward to Stalin and Voroshilov the plan for the North Pole flight, spurred on by the establishment of a base at the Pole by Russia's 'Commissar of the Ice', Dr Otto J. Schmidt.

A very considerable portion of the modern Soviet empire lies above the Arctic Circle, and since 1932 in particular the whole area had been opened up under control of what was then the Central Administration of the Northern Sea Route. Schmidt sailed on several preliminary explorations of these northern territories and in 1932 made the north-east passage from Europe to the Bering

Straits in one navigation season.

Aviation played an increasing part in these Arctic probings—scouting for ships, mapping and exploring, supply-dropping, and in the case of the sinking of the 'Chelyuskin', trapped in shifting pack ice in February 1934, taking off the entire crew and passengers marooned on the ice floes.

Schmidt's North Pole base was established and maintained entirely by aircraft, and from the meteorological station there valuable scientific data on polar weather conditions would be made available to Chkalov.

At last, Chkalov and Biadukov were summoned to Stalin's Moscow office, where also waited Molotov and Voroshilov, to put forward personally their plan. That other famous Soviet flier, Sigmund Levanevsky, was also there to present his alternative plan of a North Pole flight in a four-motor

The ANT-25 in earlier form than depicted in the general arrangement drawing. This may have been during the 1936 flight by Chkalov, Beliakov and Biadukov.

machine (he later made an ill-starred attempt which ended in disaster after engine trouble and bad weather were encountered soon after crossing the Pole).

Stalin called in Alksnis, chief of Soviet aviation, and while they were waiting for him, conversation ranged over many aspects of flying, including the valuable knowledge gained from study and purchase of U.S. aircraft and equipment.

When he arrived, Alksnis gave Chkalov the go-ahead, endorsed by Stalin and the others. Final preparations took less than three weeks, but in fact the flight was backed by two years of preliminary work by the Committee of Long Distance Flights, which was responsible for the training and teaming of record crews and development of equipment and aircraft.

A batch of the latest American charts were a valuable last-minute addition to the assorted gear bundled into the plane before the take-off on 18 June 1937. Tupolev was there to see them off. A white flag waved, and the red-winged plane began to trundle along the narrow single concrete runway. At six minutes past one the wheels lifted, Biadukov quickly retracted the landing gear, and with Chkalov at the controls the crew settled down to the flight routine, escorted on the first leg of the journey by an old twin-engined ANT-4 and another plane.

As they flew north towards the Arctic wastes, an early scare came when oil began flooding the cabin floor; eventually the cause was traced to overfilling of the system caused by over-enthusiastic pumping by the crew.

The next hazard was ice. Frantic work with the propeller de-icer cleared the prop, but ice still gathered on the wings and tail. Weighed down by the heavy fuel load, the plane inched upwards, until at 8200 feet over the Barents Sea it broke through the cloud into brilliant sunshine, and the ice began to break away.

Further tussles began with ice as the machine droned onwards over a sea of water and ice—this time the plane had to claw its way to 13,600 feet before clearing the cloud.

Slowly, monotonously, the hours slipped by. Chkalov, having spent the first eight hours at the controls, was asleep when, soon after 4 a.m. on 19 June, in brilliant sun and unlimited visibility, Biadukov and Beliakov looked down from 13,600 feet on the wilderness of fissured ice that was the Pole, distinguished only by their calculations and the sensitive whirlings of the compasses.

Past the Pole and headed south again for North America, the plane reached its 18,700 ft ceiling, cruising precariously, losing height at every bump, dodging cloud or boring into it fearful of ice.

Spasms of frenzied activity interrupted the tedium of their solitary flight; an ice blockage in the cooling system nearly seized the motor; ice caused them to inch up and down the heavens seeking clear air. But finally at 4.15 p.m. the same day; after 40 hours of flight over 3860 miles, Cape Pierce Point in the Canadian North West Territories came into view. At 6 p.m. they were over the Great Bear Lakes, and two hours later the great Mackenzie River and mountain range.

A front of storm clouds forced them to turn west towards the Rocky Mountains and the Pacific, mountains forced them higher and the oxygen supply began to give out. At 20,000 feet they had

Chkalov (centre), *Beliakov* (left) *and Baidukov immediately after landing after their 5507-mile flight from Moscow.*

to carry on with an occasional whiff of oxygen, nursing the diminishing fuel supply and fighting against the lassitude and anoxaemia.

And with the oxygen finally gone, they were forced down again until at 13,000 feet they broke cloud to see the Pacific Ocean beneath. At the expense of a four-hour diversion, the worst of the weather had been avoided and the Rockies crossed.

Turning south again down the Pacific coast, the Queen Charlotte Islands were passed. Then the sun, which had alternately blinded down or been dimmed to greyness, filtered by swirling mist and cloud, sank below the horizon. In the gathering darkness, flying blind in cloud and hail, Biadukov sat at the controls watching the instruments, the dimly-lit cabin behind littered with equipment and the bodies of his sleeping companions, feeling unutterably alone.

First the Seattle and then the Portland radio beacons guided them in. Past Portland the fuel gauges began to flicker on the 'empty' stop, so a turn was made back into the Portland beam. They eventually slipped into the soggy field at Vancouver, Washington, after 63 hours 17 minutes in the air and 5507 miles from their take-off field.

Chkalov did not break the existing long-distance record, but his flight was a true pioneering effort and set the stage for a second, successful, attempt the following month. Colonel M.M. Gromov, Commandant A.B. Youmachev, and Engineer S.A. Daniline set off from Chelkovc Airport, Moscow, in the modified ANT-25 registered NO25-1 along the route Matochkin Char, Novaya Zemlya, Rudolf Island, and the North Pole. Sixty-two hours later, having flown 6262 miles, they landed at San Jacinto, California, to set a new world's long-distance record for the Soviet Union.

Thus ended a series of flights which, apart from the prestige gained, obtained for the Russians priceless information and experience in Arctic flying and polar weather conditions. Now, the Soviets have a veritable Arctic air empire based on a network of military and meteorological stations clear across the roof of the world.

Biadukov and Beliakov had distinguished careers in the Soviet Air Force during the Second World War, each reaching Major-General's rank. The latter's 1957 comment on the flight as a Lieutenant-General of Aviation (Biadukov also reached this rank) was: 'On the wings of the ANT-25 we carried warm greetings from the Soviet people to all the people in America, the desire of Soviet people to live in peace and friendship with all peoples.'

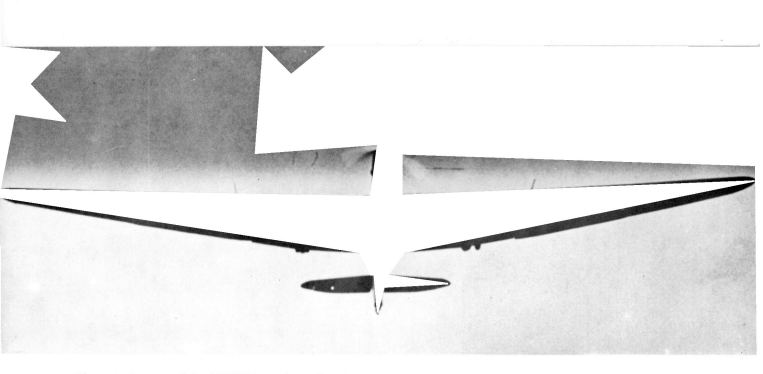

The vast wingspan of the ANT-25 is emphasised in this flying view.

Chkalov was killed on 15 December 1938 while testing a new aircraft. The son of a railroad worker (his mother was an office cleaner), he had risen to become perhaps the best-known Russian flier of the period.

Made a hero of the Soviet Union, like Chkalov, for his services to Russian aviation, Mikhail M. Gromov was born in 1899 and received his pilot's licence in 1917. After the war he led the long-distance flight from Moscow to Peking in 1925, and in 1927 worked at the Stalin Aircraft Works Plant No 1 in Moscow, having the previous year piloted an ANT-3 on a round-Europe propaganda flight. Early in the Second World War, Gromov headed a Soviet air mission to the United States to study methods of aircraft production. Back on the Russian front, he commanded a Stormovik group and finished the war as a Colonel-General. In 1946 he became Chairman of the Praesidium of the Chkalov Central Aero Club, and a year later visited England a second time as head of a Russian delegation.

The original ANT-25 was designed in 1932—it is said by order of Stalin himself—by P.O. Sukhoi under the direction of A.N. Tupolev at the Central Aero-Hydrodynamic Institute (TSAGI), Moscow. Much was made at the time of the machine's completely Russian origin as to the motor and equipment as well as the airframe, although in fact some of the instruments were of British and U.S. manufacture.

The machine was of conventional all-metal construction, spanning about 112 ft and extending 44 ft in length. Overall height was 18 ft, aspect ratio 10, wing area around 945 sq ft, wing loading 26.4 lb sq ft, and power loading, based on a normal 900-hp output, 27.7 lb/hp. Empty weight was roughly 9250 lb, but an enormous 13,000-lb fuel load—enough for over 7000 miles flight—chiefly contributed towards the 24,885-lb gross weight. Slightly differing figures were given in various contemporary sources, but all added up to the same general picture.

Power plant for the later record flight was an AM-34R 12-cylinder Vee liquid-cooled 900-1000-hp engine driving a large-diameter adjustable-pitch 3-bladed propeller, giving a top speed around 150 mph. Special attention was paid to the engine cooling system to allow fault-free cold-weather functioning.

A Russian photo shows a modified earlier version, labelled ANT-25 (RD), with a blunter nose, lower thrust line (probably with an inverted Vee engine), and tiny two-bladed propeller, but the AM-34R model was used for the North Pole flights.

Aft of the engine was the pilot's seat, over the front spar. A full complement of blind-flying instruments was provided, but no automatic pilot. The remainder of the crew's quarters comprised a long narrow cabin, with first a rough bunk, then a midships position for the navigator facing the starboard wing trailing edge, and behind him the second pilot's position with dual controls.

Navigation and radio gear was very complete and included two transmitters and a wing root-mounted receiver, radio compass (the loop for which was carried either on the roof or the belly), two aperiodic compasses, a sun compass in a small transparent canopy on the fuselage roof over the wing, and assorted chronometers and timepieces.

The ANT-25 on display at the Paris Salon.

Side-folding hoods covered the front and rear pilot positions, and the navigator had his own transparent hatch above the compartment. For emergency use on the ground, a petrol-engine generator was carried in the rear fuselage to work the radios. Other emergency gear included an inflatable rubber life raft, with flotation bags in the wing leading edge compartments. Heating was by warmed air passed over the exhaust stacks and through cabin ducts.

The wing centre section was an integral part of the fuselage structure. Attached to the stubs were long finely tapered metal-covered outer panels of ANT-6 aerofoil section, with pronounced chord-wise ribbing on upper and lower external surfaces, the whole fabric-covered, painted and lacquered to give the smoothest possible finish. Internal structure was based on a three-spar box beam, part of which formed a sealed compartmented integral fuel tank. Twin-wheeled main landing gears retracted backwards into large fairings attached to the bottom surfaces of the wing trailing edge. The tail wheel was neatly faired but non-swivelling. The tailplane was wire-braced and its incidence adjustable for trimming.

For the Chkalov flight, the machine was as illustrated in the tone general arrangement drawing. All wing and horizontal tail surfaces were painted red to make the plane visible from the air should a forced landing be made in the snow. The fuselage was silver, but with the nose and narrow stripes along the fuselage upper and lower centre lines painted a dark colour, probably black. The legend 'Stalin's Route' was painted in Russian along the fuselage.

Hero of the Soviet Union Colonel M.M. Gromov, Commandant A.B. Youmachev and Engineer S.A. Daniline in front of the ANT-25.

ROOT

0   5   10   20
FT.

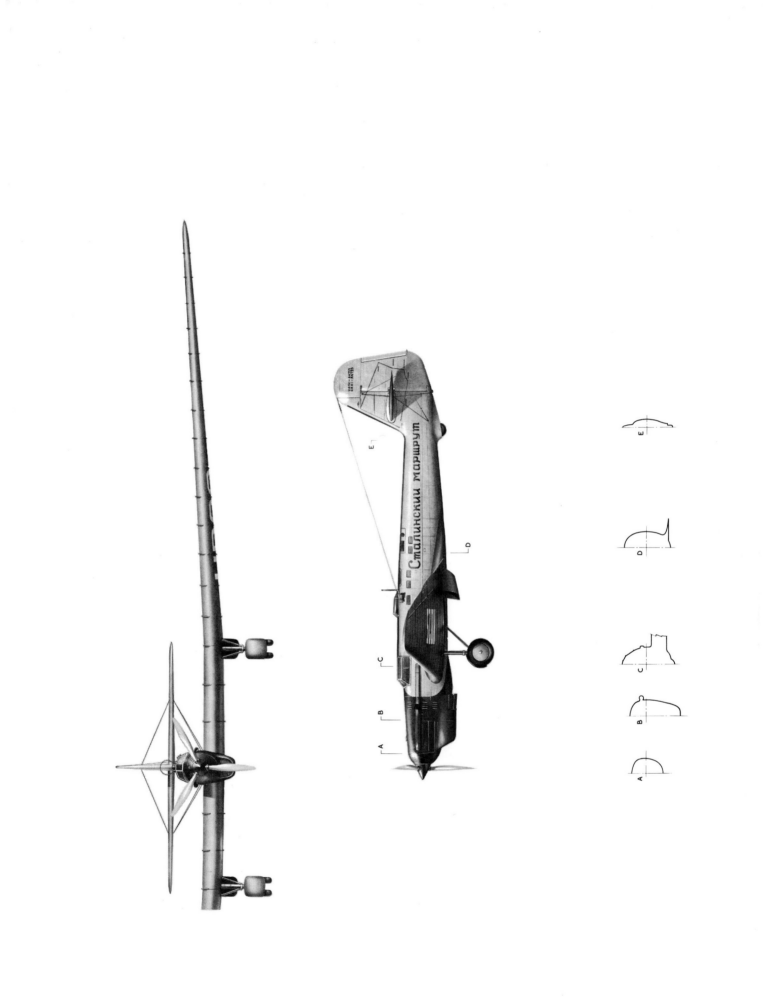

Jacqueline Cochran's Seversky AP-7

Jacqueline Cochran, winner of Bendix Trophy Race, being congratulated by Mr. Bendix.

AVIATION USED TO BE, and still is for the most part, a man's game. But from long before 1903 and the Wrights there have always been those women who challenged male supremacy in the air, often with conspicuous success. The period between the wars brought forth a succession of great airwomen, one of the most famous being Miss Jacqueline Cochran.

Jackie's first job at the age of eight was pushing a cart up and down the aisles in a Columbus cotton mill—at six cents an hour for a 12-hour night shift. Following a strike at the mills she got a job as domestic with a Jewish family of hairdressers and gradually worked her way into the business from the bottom. At 14 she took a job as permanent wave operator in a Montgomery, Ala., store, where she was taken under the wing of an influential client, began to make a circle of young friends and later bought a Model T Ford from her savings. Thus began her first experience with engines. With diversions into nursing, travelling saleswoman and partnership in a small beauty shop, Jackie finally got to New York and started making good money in a high-class beauty salon as a top operator.

She first thought of flying as a way to give wings to her restless feet, perhaps to take on country-wide representation of a good cosmetics company, and in 1932 went along to Roosevelt Field during her vacation for her first flying lesson, after which, in her own words, the beauty operator ceased to exist and the aviatrix was born.

Her tutor reckoned it would take her two to three months to get a licence. She got it within her three-week vacation. Later, bored with the slow-ness of school training, she bought her first plane, an old Gipsy-engined Travelair, and got a navy pilot acquaintance to train her the navy way.

Jackie always set her sights high. The following year, as well as starting her famous cosmetics business, she was planning to compete with top aviators from many countries in the MacRobertson England-Australia air race. She bought a Northrop Gamma, put extra fuel tanks in the mail compartment and installed a Curtiss Conqueror engine with an early-type supercharger. Supercharger failure caused two forced landings in quick succession, the second damaging the plane beyond easy repair. Casting around for a replacement plane for the race, she settled on the Granville Brothers *Q.E.D.*

A factory photograph of the Seversky AP-7 before being painted in race markings.

high-speed, long-range two-seater, and after take-off from England with co-pilot Wesley Smith flew the long hop to Bucharest, Roumania, to arrive well ahead of the rest of the field. But the plane had to stay there for repair of a number of faults that had revealed themselves during the flight, and Jackie had to return to England by boat and train.

Nothing daunted she decided next year to enter for the 1935 Bendix Trophy race and made a spectacular night take-off in fog in the Northrop Gamma, by now re-engined with a Pratt & Whitney radial. Bad weather and a vibrating overheated engine caused her to give up this race too, though she had more luck in the 1937 Bendix, flying a Beechcraft D-17 into third place at 194.7 mph.

Her biggest triumph to date, however, came in the 1938 Bendix race. Her mount was a Seversky AP-7 as featured in the tone general arrangement drawing, delivered just two days before the race and untested by her. Developed from the famous army P-35, the AP-7 was a maker's prototype of what eventually became the EP-1 model for Sweden and then the P-35A. Compared with the P-35, a more powerful Pratt & Whitney R-1830 Twin Wasp was introduced, an extra fuselage bay added near the tail and the engine moved slightly forward to compensate, giving a revised length of 26 ft 10 in instead of 25 ft 2 in. Wing area was slightly increased to 225 sq ft mainly because of much larger root fairings. The landing gear fairings were modified so that the wheels were completely enclosed by complicated hinging sections. The rear fixed portion of the canopy was cleared of metal framing and made completely transparent with Plexiglass stiffeners. Armament was omitted, of course, but full radio carried for the race. Landing lights were provided in both wings and an engine air intake added in front of the windscreen. The span remained at 36 ft Jackie's racing number '13' was carried on both sides of the fuselage and on the port wing tip upper surface and starboard tip lower surface.

Taking off along the darkened runway at 3 a.m., Jackie hauled the fuel-packed Seversky into the air and donned the new Mayo oxygen mask she was testing. As the flight progressed, it became apparent that the fuel from the right integral wing tank was not feeding properly to the engine. She had to hold that wing high to drain the tank. Later it transpired that a mysterious wad of paper had been causing the blockage. Storms forced her high and slowed the plane, and she eventually arrived at Cleveland twenty minutes later than her ETA and with three gallons of fuel left, but winner of the event at 249.7 mph. At the end of the landing roll a disgusted judge had to wait while she took out her makeup box and repaired the ravages of the gruelling flight. Following Frank Fuller's example of the year before in his Seversky SEV-S2, Jackie later took off again for Bendix, NJ, to create a new women's transcontinental west-east record at 242.1 mph. Next year she entered for the Bendix

Jacqueline Cochran sitting in Frank Sinclair's Seversky which finished fourth in the 1937 Bendix Trophy race.

The Army Corps Seversky P-35 monoplane fighter on which the AP-7 was based.

The Seversky AP-9, retaining the AP-7 fuselage but with the larger-span wing into which the undercarriage retracted completely.

again with a rebuilt machine comprising the AP-7 fuselage with the thinner, bigger-span AP-9 wing into which the revised landing gear retracted completely. She did not compete in the race after all, but later went on to set some outstanding records in the new machine.

Eventually, Jackie became America's best-known airwoman. She had a distinguished wartime career both with the British Air Transport Auxiliary and later as the chief architect of the American WASPs. Her postwar services to United States aviation, which added to her many other awards the Gold Medal of the FAI, have been no less valuable, and her competitive flights even more exciting.

But the chief impetus behind her flying career has not been the search for headlines. On every important flight she has taken aloft with her some new piece of equipment, perhaps tested a new fuel, often flown a completely untried plane, in a successful quest to add her very substantial mite to the sum of aeronautical knowledge and achievement.

E

E

O   5   10
FEET

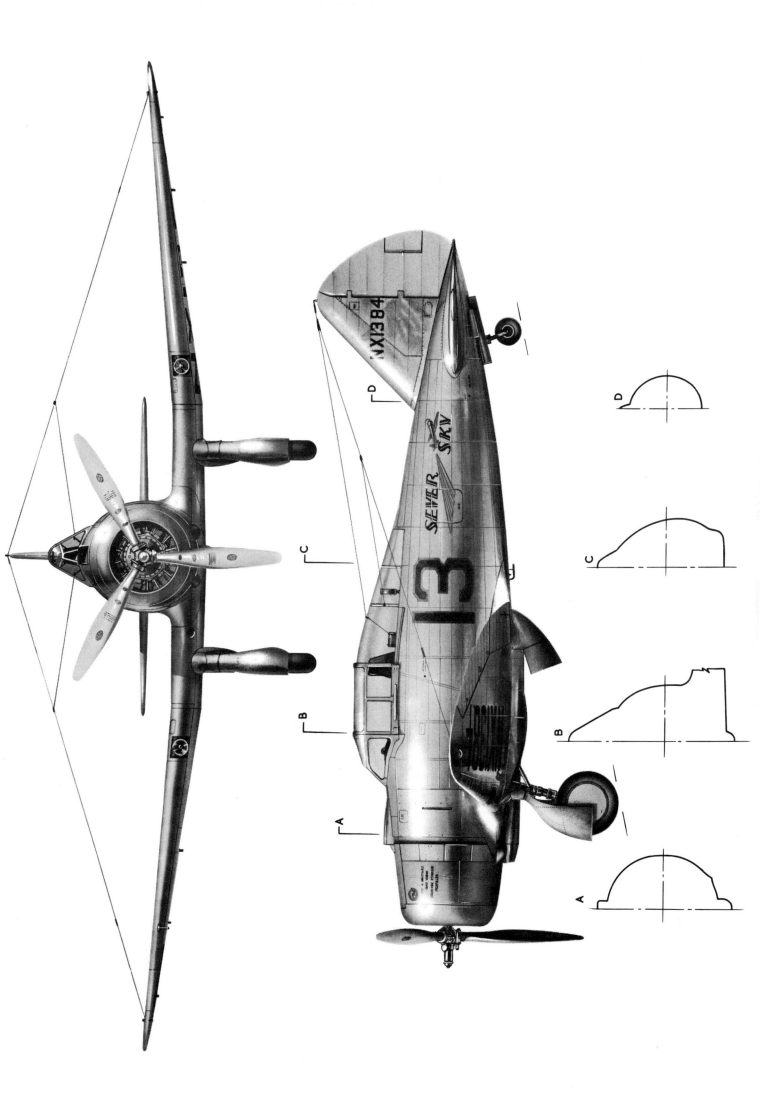

Galland's Messerschmitt Bf 109E

General of Fighters Adolf Galland

COMPARED WITH the modest scores of the leading Allied fighter pilots of the Second World War, their German counterparts exacted a ferocious toll from the various air forces against which they were pitted. Four top-scoring German aces were credited with well over 1100 victories between them, and nearly 90 lesser lights claimed over 100 (some over 200) victims apiece.

Personal claims in any extensive air action tend to be exaggerated for well-known reasons, despite meticulous care on the part of interrogating personnel. During the Battle of Britain, British pilots' claims were exaggerated by more than 50 per cent, while, for their part, the Germans claimed roughly 3½ times as many British machines as were actually destroyed. Later, USAAF bomber crews raiding over Europe in perfectly good faith claimed so many victims in a few months that the whole German fighter arm should have ceased to exist.

Assuming a good margin of optimism, German Second World War personal scores nevertheless were impressive. In 1939 and the first half of 1940 the Luftwaffe had easy pickings from a succession of opponents who numerically or qualitatively, or both, were far inferior, and the same story was repeated in Russia in 1941.

After the first flush of victories the German aircrews, increasingly outnumbered, were often obliged to fly for much longer periods of operational duty, at least in some categories and on some fronts, than was customary during the same period on the Allied side. Thus individuals were able to accumulate impressive victory scores while at the same time running proportionally higher risks of eventual mental and physical collapse, injury or death.

One of the greatest personalities, the self-styled *enfant terrible,* of the *Luftwaffe* was Generalmajor Adolf Galland, ace with over 100 victories and for much of the war General of Fighters. His prestige and force of character allowed him to cross swords even with Goering concerning the planning and use of the Fighter Arm with which Galland bitterly disagreed on many occasions. The Fighter Arm was the Cinderella of the *Luftwaffe*, according to Galland, with low priorities for equipment and personnel. As a fighting commander, Galland never wielded the political power to alter a series of what

A captured example of the Messerschmitt B 109.

he considered were wrong decisions taken by the High Command and by Hitler himself.

Galland first flew—as a glider pilot—in 1928. Later, he was one of very few accepted for pilot training with *Lufthansa,* the German state airline, within which were sown the seeds of the new undercover air force. As part of the *Lufthansa* training, he received a clandestine fighter course, continued during a tour of military training with the Italian air force.

In 1935, when the security curtain was finally raised on a *Luftwaffe* already in being, Galland joined the reborn Richthofen Fighter Group, flying He 51s, and two years later went to Spain to fight with the German Condor Legion. Here he flew He 51s mainly on ground attack missions and first used his squadron insignia, a Mickey Mouse emblem. During a year-long tour fighting with Franco he flew over 300 sorties before being recalled to Germany to advise on ground support tactics.

He managed to achieve a long-cherished transfer to the Fighter Arm after the victorious 1939 Polish campaign, the assault on France and the Low Countries in 1940 finding him operations officer with a fighter group flying Bf 109s. In one of these machines he gained his first air victory, over a Belgian Hurricane, on 12 May 1940.

Promoted to command a wing of the 26th Fighter Group (JG 26), on 24 July he led his unit over the Thames Estuary for its first engagement in what the Germans termed the 'second phase' of the Battle of Britain.

A short radius of action, perhaps the main fault of the Bf 109, contributed to the defeat of the *Luftwaffe* in that epic struggle, and early on Galland was in opposition to the leadership regarding the tactical use of the escorting fighters.

In an attempt to inject fresh blood into the fighter force leadership and new heart into its personnel, Goering adapted a First World War idea and promoted the best of his young fighter aces to

Introduction of the more powerful Daimler-Benz DB 605A engine giving 1475 hp was the main change on the Bf 109G, in service late in 1942.

positions of senior command. Galland and the great Werner Mölders were created fighter group commodores, leading their units into combat in person—as did Richthofen in the First World War. Ideas put forward by the new commodores more often than not fell on deaf ears at Supreme Headquarters and so began the split of opinion between Galland and Goering which widened into a gulf as the war progressed.

In preparation for the 1941 attack on Russia, German fighter groups were gradually withdrawn to the East, until only two groups, including Galland's, remained to face a growing offensive from the RAF. Mölders went to the Russian Front, where he did so well that, after attaining 100 victories, he was recalled and made General of Fighters. After his death in an air accident, Galland stepped into his shoes. He inherited a weapon which had already had the fine edge taken off it in the Battle of Britain and now had been sadly blunted in the interests of the army during the war in Russia.

The first big operation under his leadership was the Channel dash in February 1942, under the noses of the British, of the *Scharnhorst, Gneisenau, Prinz Eugen* and attendant vessels to German ports. By a fluke the flotilla evaded three separate British airborne radar patrols. Next day, Galland used 250 fighters in relays in bad weather to beat off constant British air attacks. The only serious damage to the German fleet was from mines.

Later on the same year, Galland's thorniest problem began to develop as USAAF bombers started to range in daylight over occupied Europe. Against these raids, fighters were frittered away as Goering frantically attempted to bar Allied planes from the heart of the Reich. Priority still went to bomber production for retaliation, and urgently needed fighter replacements were converted instead as fighter-bombers, night fighters, even fast reconnaissance aircraft. Galland instigated the 'wing' attack by massed formations of fighters, clamoured for the new jet machines under development, created 'storm' wings of picked pilots flying specially-armed machines, tried out new weapons, three times created with tremendous effort a fighter reserve, only to have it seized and whittled away in some abortive enterprise. But never did he gain political assent to push his policies through to fruition.

Finally, after constant friction with his superiors, Galland was relieved of his post in January 1945, an event which caused a near mutiny among the fighter personnel he had championed. Shorn of high office, he nevertheless was too valuable an officer to discard and was chosen to form a picked unit to fly the long-delayed Me 262 jet fighter. Developed in good time and produced in large numbers, these machines, he knew, could materially have altered the air situation over Germany with their 120-mph speed advantage over the fastest Allied types, heavy four-cannon armament, and the deadly 5-cm R4M air-to-air rockets. He finished the war commanding

JV 44, the jet-equipped 'Experts Unit'.

During the Battle of Britain, Galland flew the Bf 109E, at that time sharing with the Spitfire the reputation of being the best fighter flying. Galland rated the Spitfire 10-15 mph slower, though tighter in the turn, than the Bf 109E, and the 316-mph Hurricane I inferior on several counts, especially above 18,000 ft.

The general arrangement drawing shows how Galland's Bf 109E looked late in 1940. The basic camouflage scheme for the upper surfaces of wing, tailplane and fuselage was a 'splinter' pattern in two shades of dark green and black-green, with undersurfaces and the sides and bottom of the fuselage finished in a light blue shade. The fuselage sides were mottled with a paint spray of light grey-green. Engine cowling and rudder were over-painted bright yellow for easy identification of the unit's machines in the air. On the fuselage sides were the JG 26 'Schlageter' wing insignia (a black 'S' on a white shield), Galland's Mickey Mouse emblem in black and white (on the port side only) and the white-outlined black arrowhead and bars denoting the Wing 1A or operations officer flying an aircraft belonging to the second Group in the Wing. The green spinner denoted a staff or head-quarters flight aircraft and on the rudder were red and black bars detailing Galland's victory score.

A captured Bf 109E test-flown by the British

Considerable refinement of the aerodynamic features were incorporated on the F version of the Bf 109. Top speed was increased to 380-90 mph.

Air Ministry achieved the following performance. Top speed was 354 mph at 14,760 ft; initial climb 3100 ft per min; service ceiling 36,000 ft; absolute ceiling 37,500 ft; range 560 miles at 248 mph. Armament was two 20-mm cannon in the wings and two 7.9-mm (.310 in) machine-guns beneath the engine top cowling. Power plant was a Mercedes-Benz DB 601A inverted 'V', liquid-cooled with direct fuel injection and giving 985 hp for take-off. Span was about 32 ft 4 in; length 28 ft 2 in; wing area 174 sq ft; empty weight 4360 lb; loaded weight 5400 lb.

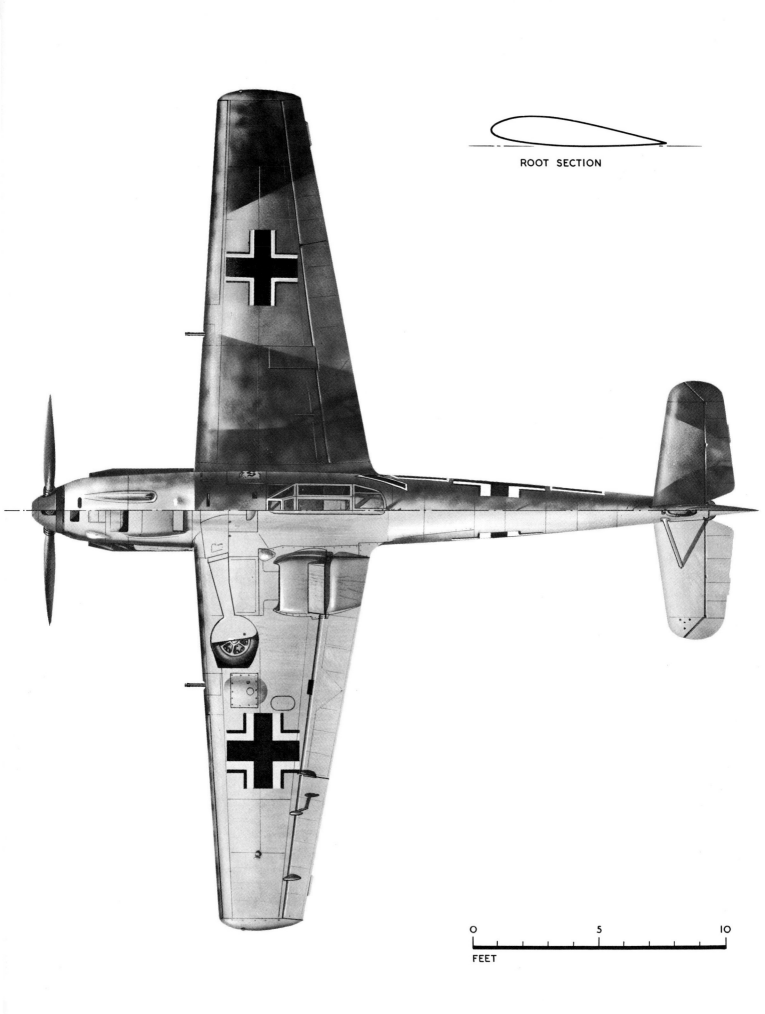

ROOT SECTION

0   5   10
FEET

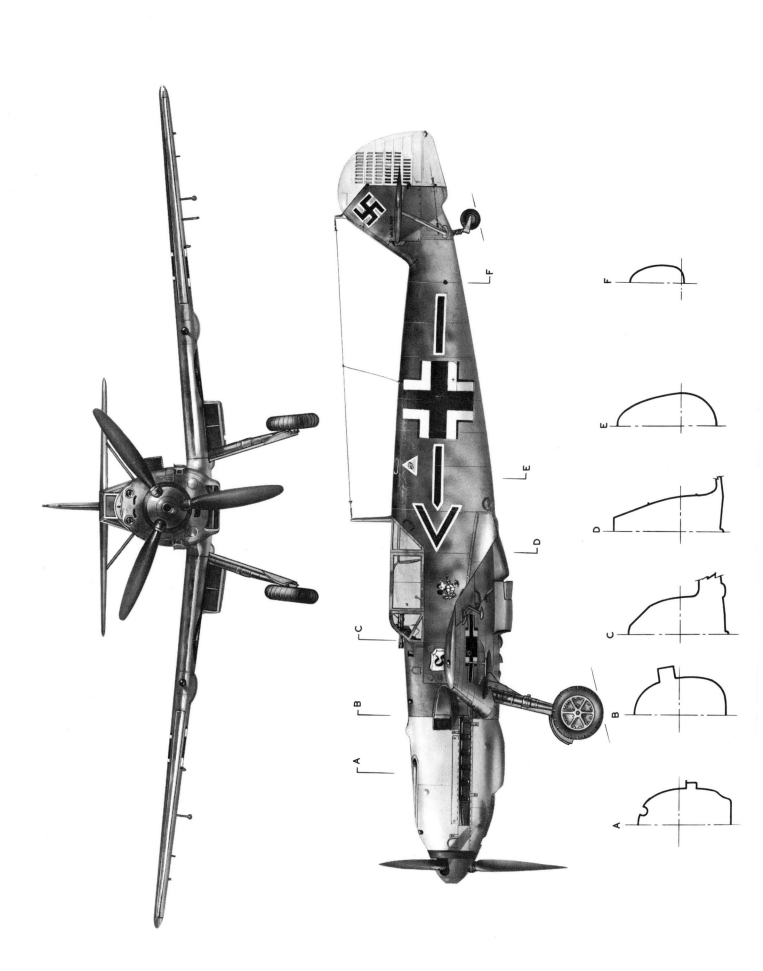

Bader's Spitfire

Bader seated on the Hurricane which he flew with No. 242 Squadron.

ON A CRISP DECEMBER DAY in 1931 at Woodley aerodrome, near Reading, Berkshire, three Bristol Bulldog fighters from Number 23 Squadron, RAF, were trundling out on to the grass, bumping along the turf with rudders gently wagging. One by one they took off watched by a group of Reading Aero Club members, who good-naturedly had been chaffing one of the RAF pilots on his aerobatic prowess. Apparently he must have been nettled, for suddenly one of the Bulldogs banked round, pointed its snub nose towards the clubhouse and commenced a low pass across the airfield, Jupiter engine roaring. The hurtling plane started a slow roll and, dismayed, the onlookers saw the heavy fighter sink. Suddenly a wing-tip touched the ground and in an instant the machine cartwheeled and disintegrated into a cloud of dust and flying debris.

The stunned spectators raced across the aerodrome towards the smoking wreckage and quickly began to extricate the pilot. His face battered, ribs broken, legs mangled, and weak with loss of blood, Pilot Officer Douglas Robert Stewart Bader probably would have but a few hours to live.

But Bader refused to die. And later, with both legs amputated, one completely and the other at the knee, he refused to accept the limitations which two artificial limbs would surely impose on anyone. Reluctanctly settled in an office job with Shell—he had already mastered flying an aeroplane again and driving a car before being invalided out of flying duties with the RAF—he gradually acquired skill as a golfer, oddly enough more difficult for him than piloting or driving.

Still, the desk job rankled, and with the coming of war in 1939 and the Air Ministry more inclined to cut red tape that had previously prevented him from resuming flying duties, he argued his way in front of an RAF Volunteer Reserve Medical Board. The President of the Board, impressed by his enthusiasm and determination, persuaded the doctors to send him for another flying test at the Central Flying School. This passed successfully, there followed a refresher course to master new features, variable-pitch airscrews, retractable landing gear and increased instrumentation that had appeared on service aircraft during the eight years since his crash. Finally, he managed a posting to a Spitfire squadron commanded by an old RAF colleague.

The prototype Spitfire, K5054, in flight.

This was the time of the 'phoney war', with Germany lying in wait in front of the Maginot Line. The 'Spit' had yet to prove itself in battle, though judged the finest fighter of its day, and squadron sorties were confined to convoy escort over the Channel and like duties.

Then came the German invasion of the Low Countries and France. Bader was a flight leader now, and made his own first kill, a Bf 109, over the beaches of Dunkirk.

In the lull after Dunkirk, Bader was promoted to lead a Canadian Hurricane squadron, 242, which had been mauled in the bitter air fight in France. Quickly Bader had the Canadians worked up to top morale, chafing at the bit as they watched the neighbouring Southern Group 11 become progressively engaged with massed enemy formations in the opening phases of the Battle of Britain. Fighter Command could not show its hand too soon; there had to be a reserve behind the battling Southern squadrons, and 242's 12 Group were ranged to ward off air blows at the Midlands' vital industrial areas.

But one day, Bader exultantly at their head, 242 were drawn into the vortex of the battle. New tactics and techniques—the dive into the midst of an enemy formation to scatter it, the combined handling of three, even five, fighter squadrons under a single leader—sprang from Bader's fertile brain during the ensuing weeks. Not always was he right, but fighter tactics during the battle, and afterwards when Fighter Command began to take the offensive, owed much to his imagination and combat experience.

Gradually the great air battles over England died away. Goering was beaten, the invasion postponed. And early the following year began the first offensive sweeps by an RAF grown strong enough to challenge the *Luftwaffe* over its own occupied territory. Bader, now a Wing Commander, went to Tangmere to organise a three-squadron wing (Numbers 145, 610 and 616) for the new role.

As the sweeps probed into France, sanguinary air fighting developed as the defending Messerschmitts came up to give battle. Bader's personal score began to mount again. The bloodthirsty brand of confidence which had infused 242 Squadron now pervaded the Tangmere wing, and even Bader's wife came to think of him as bullet-proof, invulnerable.

But on 9 August 1941, it had to be broken to her that Douglas Bader was missing. He had taken his Wing across the Channel, where during an aerial engagement he had collided with an enemy fighter and parachuted to earth, in the process losing one of his artificial legs and damaging the other.

Bader still tried to wage war in captivity by attempted escapes and by tormenting his jailers. After the war he finished his service career as Group Captain with most of the high decorations, including the D.S.O and D.F.C. with bars, Chevalier of the Legion of Honour, and the Croix de Guerre with Palm. His personal score was 22½ enemy planes confirmed but this record, although meritorious, did not reflect the main achievements of his war career. More important were the impact of his irrepressible spirit and courage on service and public morale, and of his keen mind on tactics.

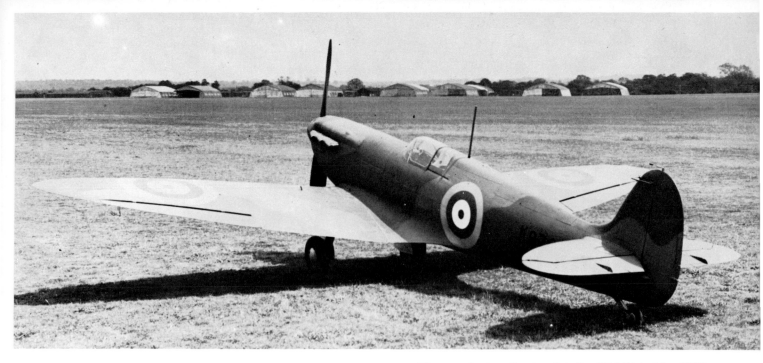

The very first production Spitfire, K9787, in May 1938. A great deal of the early testing and developement work was done with this machine, which eventually ended up with a photo-reconnaisance unit.

Spitfire Is of No. 65 Fighter Squadron based at the time at Hornchurch. The machine in the foreground is flown by another great British ace, Flying Officer (later Wing Commander) R.R.S. Tuck.

The influence of his personality and example has continued into peacetime. In 1955 Bader was made a Commander of the Order of the British Empire (C.B.E) for his work in inspiring other handicapped people to overcome their disabilities. Wherever he goes on business he makes a point of looking up those who have to surmount the same misfortunes. He insists that his war record is hardly of unusual merit; but the mastery of his steel legs, his stubborn, tenacious fight to be as whole men, his brilliant leadership, and the inspiration his example affords to countless handicapped thousands the world over, surely are.

Bader flew both the great British fighters of the period. Over Dunkirk he piloted the Spitfire I; during the Battle of Britain the Hurricane; at Tangmere the Spitfire IIA and IIB, and then the VA and VB.

The early Spitfire Is that he flew had eight .303 Browning machine-guns, did around 362 mph on 1310-1440 hp (combat rating) from the great-hearted Rolls-Royce Merlin II or III, rolled at 14 degrees a second at 400 mph, had a wing area and loading of 242 sq ft and 24 lb/sq ft, climbed to 20,000 ft in 9.4 minutes, had a combat range of 395 miles and normally weighed about 5280 lb.

The Spitfire IIA and IIB had the 1175-hp (1280 combat) Merlin XII running on 100-octane fuel, were armed with eight Brownings, or four Browning and two Oerlikon-Hispano cannon, respectively. Armor plate (73 lb), bullet-proof windscreen, self-sealing tanks (shared with later MK Is) and a three-bladed Rotol constant-speed airscrew were fitted.

Early in 1941, the new MK V version began to reach the squadrons. Main change was the motor, Merlin series 45, 46, 50, 55 and 56 being fitted during the production run, giving combat ratings from 1415 to 1585 hp at various boosts and altitudes. Top speed was raised to around 375 mph at 21,500 ft on the fastest model. Fuselage longerons were reinforced, armour weight increased to 129 lb (VA) or 152 lb (VB), and late aircraft had metal ailerons which made aileron control much lighter. The VA still carried eight Brownings, the VB two cannon and four Brownings; the VC had a new 'universal' design of wing which could accommodate either of these armament combinations, or four Hispano cannon.

A cannon-armed Spitfire V of the type which equipped the Tangmere wing.

Bader favoured the machine-gun armament and was flying a VA, while most of his wing had VBs, when he was forced down in August 1941. The tone three-view drawing depicts as nearly as can be ascertained how his VA looked on that day. As a wing commander he had the privilege of putting his initials on the side of the machine in place of the regular squadron code letters, so that his plane could be recognised and rallied upon during the after combat.

Royal Air Force camouflage at this period was in a dark green and dark brown (earth) pattern on the upper surfaces, with a pastel shade of blue-green (officially Sky Type S, or 'duck-egg green') on the undersurfaces. The spinner and an 18-in band round the rear fuselage were also Sky Type S. Bader's machine carried the serial W3185 in 1¼-in thick letters on the rear fuselage, and a wing commander's pennant (royal blue V, light blue ground, two red bars) below the windscreen Fuselage roundels were blue (outer), white and red, surrounded by a yellow circle; top wing roundels were blue (outer) and red; and normal blue-white-red roundels were on the wing under-surfaces. Fin stripes were red (leading), white, blue. Bader's initials were probably repeated in black below the motor cowling nose. Airscrew was dull black with 4-in matt yellow tips. Black ¾-in lines were painted along the wing forward upper surfaces, and fore and aft on the port wing inboard at rib no 4, to indicate walkway boundaries. Trestle points, stenciled notices, etc. were black. The letters 'DB' on the fuselage sides were grey and since this was a presentation aircraft the inscription 'Lord Lloyd I' was painted in white script lettering on the starboard fuselage side just below the windscreen.

Figures for the VA were: span 36 ft 10 in; length 29 ft 11 in; height 11 ft 5 in; wing area 242 sq ft.

Cannon-armed Spitfire VBs in formation.

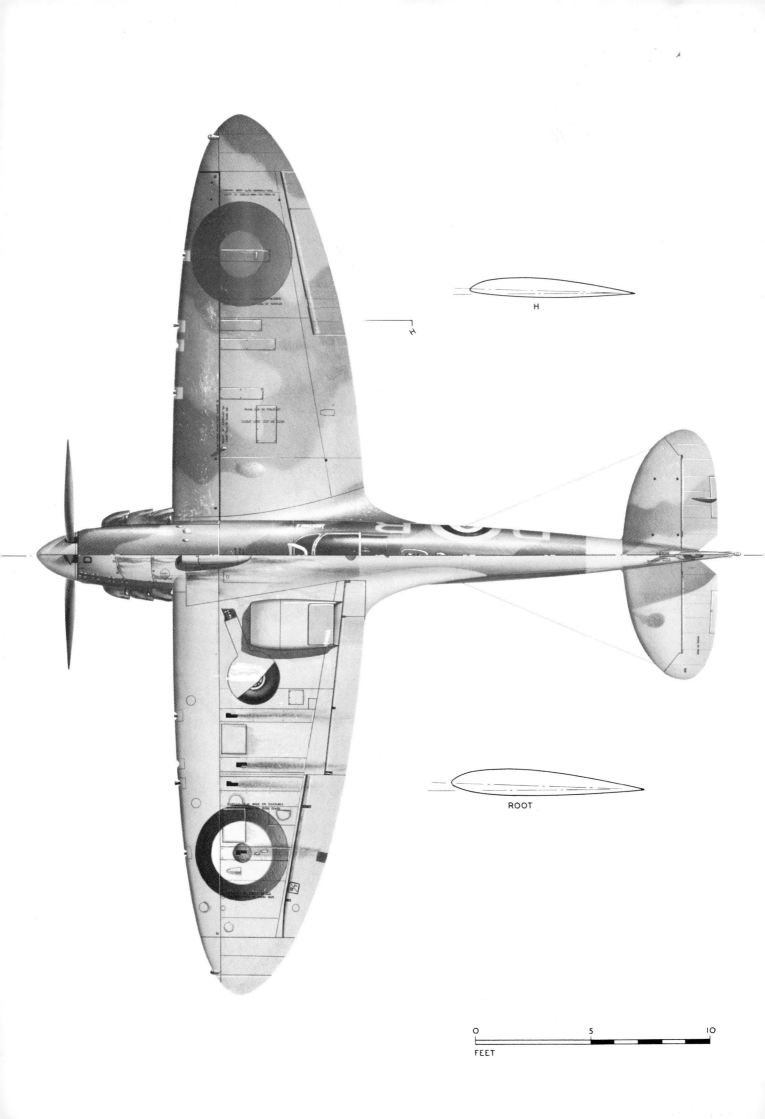

H

ROOT

0   5   10

FEET

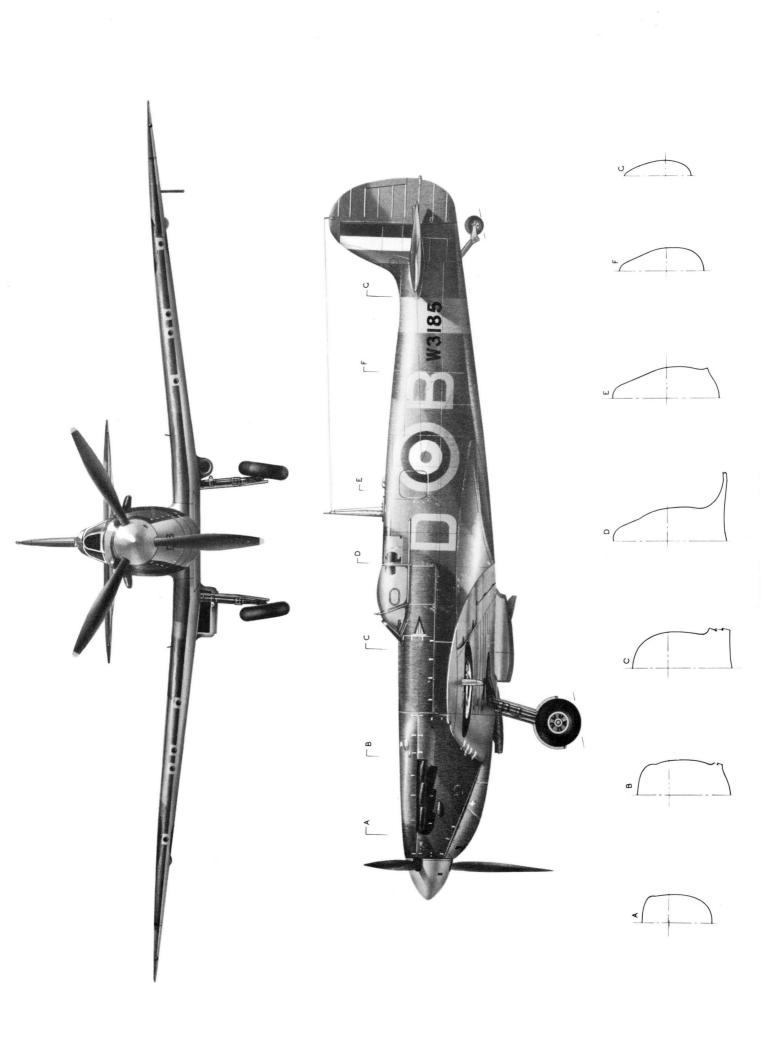

Chennault's 'Flying Tigers'

Chennault shows off the "Flying Tigers" emblem on his jacket.

'THE BILLY MITCHELL OF PURSUIT' is what John Hersey called Major-General Claire Lee Chennault, leader of the legendary 'Flying Tigers', the American Volunteer Group fighting the Japanese in Burma and China in 1941-42. In the lean years for military aviation following the First World War Chennault, like Mitchell, found himself in continual opposition to what he felt was a hidebound High Command which still considered the aeroplane to be an auxiliary to the conventional ground and naval armed forces. This was contrary to the views of an expanding group of air officers and aviation strategists of many nations who recognised the possibilities of military aviation as a vital new and independent arm able to play a decisive role in a future major conflict.

Chennault considered also that too big a proportion of the modest air force funds available were being spent on perfecting the bomber, to the detriment of the fighter arm. He had missed the First World War, graduating as a 'pursuit' pilot in 1919. He revelled in the power and agility of the fighter plane and later became a skilled Air Corps aerobatic team leader, but he could find little to enthuse over in the organisation and training with its text-book flying and outdated tactics. He had some highly original theories to contribute to the science of fighter aviation. He broke down the problems of the fighter's role into three basic ingredients, detection, interception and destruction, and advanced solutions to meet all of them.

Regarding detection and interception, in the days long before radar he advocated a nationwide network of observation and tracking posts reporting to filter centres and plotting rooms, where the route, strength and probable destination of a raiding aerial formation could be ascertained and defending fighters alerted and briefed for interception. Such ideas approximated to the British pre-radar air defence network of ground observers and persists in the modern USAF as the Ground Observer Corps to augment the vast early-warning radar network.

Concerning destruction of the raiders, Chennault was an advocate of heavier armament for fighters to counter-balance the increasing defensive fire of the 'aerial battleship' type of heavy bomber experimented with by the Air Service (later the Air

Chocks away for an AVG P-40 off on an intercepting mission. Note the fuselage and wing guns and the windscreen armoured glass panel.

Corps) and in squadron service eventually with the Russian and French Air Forces. Experimental four- and six-gun fighters were flown in 1931/32 in the U.S.A., but the standard armament for American fighters remained two fixed synchronised machine-guns until shortly before the Second World War.

Chennault is also credited with evolving loose 'finger tip' ('finger four' in RAF parlance) fighting formations of two two-plane elements long before the Germans introduced them during the Spanish Civil War. It would be interesting to discover whether the Germans got their ideas from papers published under Chennault's name or whether they were common knowledge, such as might be current among advanced thinkers in any international band of professionals, be they scientists, doctors or air force officers. Certainly the two-plane team fighter tactics came to be used almost universally during the Second World War and after.

Impatience with the conservatism of some senior officers probably damaged Claire Chennault's career and hastened his retirement from the Air Corps in 1937, suffering from partial deafness and bronchial trouble and mentally exhausted by a years-long tussle to obtain recognition for his new ideas on 'pursuit' tactics. Yet he was shortly to obtain a unique opportunity to put many of his theories into practice, in the service of a country far from his native U.S.A.

Military flying in China reflected the turbulent internal conditions in that unhappy country, with many small air forces maintained by provincial warlords as well as by the Central Government. Chiang Kai-shek's air force was put on a regular and efficient basis by an unofficial U.S. air mission in 1932-34. After the withdrawal of that mission under Japanese diplomatic pressure, Chiang Kai-shek obtained help where he could, from Italy, Germany, Russia, Britain and other countries, with the result that by 1937 the Chinese Air Force under the nominal leadership of Madame Chiang comprised an astonishing assortment of aeroplanes, many of dubious military value and of all nation-alities, flown by foreign mercenaries as well as Chinese aircrews.

Claire Chennault was offered, and accepted, a civilian post in China as advisor on air training, and when open war with Japan broke out in 1937 he became director of air combat training and virtually second-in-command, after the Chiang Kai-sheks, of some 100 battleworthy planes. Despite considerable infusions of aid from the Soviet Union with planes and 'volunteer' pilots, the Chinese were powerless to challenge Japan's

A taxying A.V.G. P-40 with gaping shark's maw and Chinese insignia beneath the wings.

mastery of the airspace over the mainland, though the Japanese were forced to introduce their most modern bombers escorted by the new Mitsubishi A5M monoplane fighters to maintain their superiority.

The Sino-Japanese 'incident' was the forgotten war of the 'thirties, especially when war broke out in Europe in 1939. This catastrophe brought the United States to full realisation of her isolated position, bereft of major allies, and caused her to bring succour to the nations battling the Axis powers and to China, whose resistance to Japanese aggression had long been admired in North America.

In four years of war Japanese forces had virtually sealed off the Chinese interior from the main coastal ports, and Russian supplies were cut off eventually due to that country's invasion by the Germans in 1941. The aid which the U.S.A now wished to send could reach China only along the tortuous road through the mountains from Lashio, Burma, to Kunming, and this was under aerial attack by Japanese air forces as were many Chinese cities.

Over 300 aircraft were promised to Chiang Kai-shek as well as American key personnel and facilities for training Chinese pilots in the U.S.A., but direct defence by American operational squadrons could not be provided to safeguard these supplies since at the time, late 1941, the United States was not at war with Japan and had no intention of forcing such a conflict, near though it might seem.

In this favourable climate for co-operation Chennault journeyed to the U.S.A to advocate his ideas for an American volunteer force flying American planes to protect the Burma Road

supply route and Chinese cities from air attack. Not without difficulty he obtained provisional agreement from the White House for the recruitment and equipping of such a force, notwithstanding the fact that the U.S.A needed every plane and man for her own expanding forces and for aid to the embattled Allies. The pilots and ground crews were recruited from the army, navy and marine air services with promise of excellent pay, adventure and an early chance to get to grips with the potential enemy. So as not to compromise American neutrality, recruiting was done under a nominal cloak of secrecy. Personnel had to resign their U.S. commissions and sign on with the 'Central Aircraft Manufacturing Co.' of New York (owned jointly by Curtiss-Wright and the International Company of China which operated an aircraft manufacturing organisation in China) as civilian mercenaries employed by the Chinese air force. Pilots got 600 dollars a month and a 500-dollar bonus for every Japanese plane they shot down.

The American Volunteer Group, about 100 pilots (40 from the army and the rest from the navy and marines) and 150 ground-crewmen, sailed from San Fransisco on neutral ships in 1941. They reached Rangoon in September and assembled at a training base lent by the RAF at Toongoo, 300 miles up-country. There they saw several of the American Hawk H-81A fighters they would fly. The H-81A was an export version, supplied to the Royal Air Force as the Tomahawk II, of the Curtiss P-40 fighter, the U.S. Army Air Force equivalent of the Spitfire and Messerschmitt Bf 109. Rugged in build and extremely manoeuvrable, the Tomahawk had proved unacceptable as a European front-line fighter because of the insuf-

The difficulties of field maintenance in the China-Burma theatre are shown in this photograph of a P-40E with the engine cowling off.

ficient power and comparatively low-altitude rating of its Allison engine. Hurriedly ordered into service as the P-40 to equip a rapidly expanding Army Air Corps, it was neither intended for nor suited to the optimum combat heights of 18-20,000 feet which became the norm in the European air battles of 1939-40, and later was allocated by the RAF for low-altitude fighter reconnaissance or sent abroad to combat theatres, North Africa for example, where it could fight on equal terms with the opposing forces.

One hundred Tomahawks destined for the RAF were released to the American Volunteer Group, about 85-90 eventually arriving for assembly at Rangoon airport, but obtaining spares and adequate servicing was a nightmare. In November 1941 Chennault reported that only 43 planes were serviceable and 84 pilots fit for combat duty; always he had to contend with lack of certain types of spares (engines were in good supply) and replacement aircraft, so that on occasion he was hard put to it to maintain even a bare minimum of operational aircraft.

The Group was formed into three squadrons, the

1st (Adam and Eve), 2nd (Panda Bears) and 3rd (Hell's Angels), with appropriate insignia. In mid-December, two squadrons moved to Kunming in China to start operations in defence of the Burma Road and south-western Chinese cities. There they fought their first big action with the Japanese on 20 December 1941.

The American service pilots were as good as any flying with any force, but they were heavily outnumbered by skilful and disciplined Japanese airmen backed by up to ten years combat experience and flying excellent modern machines. That the Americans almost immediately attained a remarkable superiority over the enemy in their air battles can be attributed almost entirely to Chennault. During his service in China he had taken every opportunity to gather information on Japanese aircraft, personnel and air tactics. Thus he had a unique knowledge of the enemy his Group would meet and passed this information on to them in intensive ground instruction and air drills. He also taught them the combat tactics he had worked out over the past years, including the looser formations based on two-plane co-operating

A few examples of an improved version of the P-40, the P-40E, were supplied to the A.V.G. before it disbanded. Note the bomb steadying struts beneath the fuselage.

sections, sometimes with the addition of a third man as top cover. He told them how to use the good points of the P-40—its solid build, superior level and diving speed, substantial armour and fuel tank protection and usually heavier armament compared with the Japanese fighters, which had no armour and only token tank protection.

He warned them ceaselessly of the certain fatality of 'dogfighting' with or trying to outclimb or otherwise out-manoeuvre the lightly loaded Claudes, Nates and Zekes; instilled in them how to make a quick firing pass and then break away in a flat-out dive which the light Japanese machines could not sustain, until out of distance of the enemy the P-40s could zoom aloft to gain the height advantage and choose the best moment for another attack. Similar tactics became common in U.S. fighter units throughout the Pacific theatre during the rest of the war; they were suited to the characteristics of most of the American fighter aircraft and enabled their pilots to accumulate some astonishing ratios of kills to losses against the Japanese.

Another important facet of the AVG's success was the widespread radio and field telephone early-warning network Chennault, true to his theories, had set up long before 1941. Spotters along the main bombing routes and even inside Japanese-dominated territory near the enemy air bases sent in sighting reports so that Chennault had early knowledge of a raid, could track its progress and ascertain the target, and order up his fighters in good time to make an interception. British radar was a help until it was withdrawn with retreating British forces, but of course there were times when all warning systems failed and in fact many AVG aircraft were destroyed on the ground. Nevertheless, in 6½ months the Group shot down 286 enemy planes confirmed for the loss of less than fifty fighters and eight AVG pilots killed and four missing in air actions.

The American Volunteer Group contracts ran out on 4 July 1942 and the original unit broke up. Most of the personnel were incensed at what was considered the shabby treatment of their commanding officer by the U.S. Army Air Force, which now took over responsibility for the unit. Some were war-weary and eager to get home on leave; many wanted to rejoin the AAF, navy or marines now that America was in the war; still others took well-paid jobs with China National Airways or in India with the Hindustan Aircraft Co., often flying the dangerous aerial supply route over the 'Hump'. Twenty agreed to stay on temporarily with the pilots of the AAF 23rd Fighter Group, which took over from the AVG and retained their 'Flying Tiger' and 'shark's-mouth' markings, until that unit was up to strength. Chennault stayed on to command the China Air Task Force activated on the same day, 4 July, and was promoted Major-General when the CATF was expanded in the U.S. 14th Air Force on 4 March 1943. In the fighter units of these successive organisations the spirit and traditions of the 'Flying Tigers' lived on.

The AVG Hawk H-81A-3 (British Tomahawk IIB) illustrated in the general arrangement drawing was in the basic RAF camouflage markings of the period, dark brown and dark green 'shadow shading' on fuselage, tail and the upper surfaces, with a pastel greeny-blue, officially 'Sky Type S', on all undersurfaces. On the nose was the familiar 'shark's-mouth' marking, used also by the British Number 112 fighter squadron in North Africa as well as other units. The lips were black, the tongue red and the teeth white, painted over the basic finish so that the inside of the 'mouth' remained in

P-40Es of the 23rd Fighter Group, A.A.F., which took over the duties and traditions of the American Voluteer Group.

camouflage colours. The eye was white with a red pupil. Chinese air force insignia as shown were a fairly light blue and white carried on top and bottom surfaces of both wings. On the fuselage side is painted the Group emblem of a winged tiger in appropriate colouring. When the USAAF took over, this insignia changed in detail, and later on individual squadron insignia were often added.

This machine, probably of the 1st, 'Adam and Eve', squadron, had the number 14 painted in white on both sides of the fuselage and also just aft of the spinner, and the small serial number P-8127 was carried on both sides of the fin. A narrow band round the rear fuselage was painted in the squadron colour, probably white in this instance. However, the question of squadron colours and machine markings is complicated because Chennault frequently had them changed in order to create the impression of a much larger air force than the handful of planes he was in fact operating, a ruse which was completely successful in hoodwinking the Japanese. The markings of P-8127 are probably as carried early on in the unit's operation life; later on distinctive squadron emblems were

carried on the fuselage sides as well as or instead of the 'Flying Tigers' insignia.

The AVG Curtiss H-81A-3s had increased armament, self-sealing fuel tanks and armour protection as dictated by British combat experience. A Tomahawk II (P-40B) carefully tested by the RAF achieved the following performance: maximum speed 331 mph at 15,500 ft; best climb rate 1960 fpm fairly constant from ground level to 13,500 ft; climb to 10,000 ft in 5 min, to 15,000 ft in 7.7 min, to 20,000 ft in 10.8 min; service ceiling 31,400 ft; absolute ceiling 32,300 ft; range and endurance 665 miles (2.8 hours) at 20,000 ft at 1800 rpm at 234 mph; loaded weight as tested 7646 lb. The engine was a single-stage mechanically supercharged Allison V-1710-C15 giving 1090 hp at 3000 maximum rpm at 13,200 ft. Armament was two synchronised .5-inch machine-guns in the nose plus four free-firing .303-inch guns in the wings. Dimensions were: span 37 ft 3½ in; length 31 ft 8½ in; height 13 ft 2 in over airscrew arc; wing area 232 sq ft gross.

F

F

0   5   10
FEET

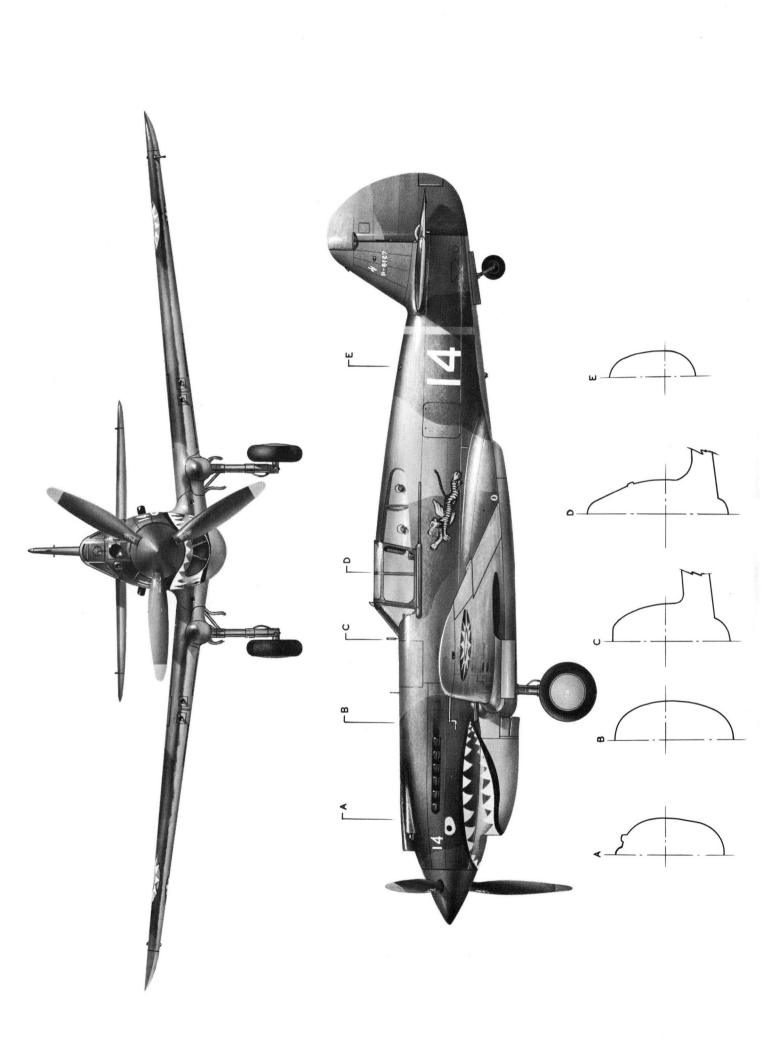

Robert Johnson's P-47 Thunderbolt

Captain Robert S. Johnson in the cockpit of his Thunderbolt fighter. Note the victory symbols painted on the aircraft's side, the armoured glass panel inside the windscreen, the reflector gun sight and the rear view mirror.

THE 'JUG', 'T-BOLT', 'ACE–MAKER', 'seven-ton milk bottle', these were some of the names they called the rugged P-47 Thunderbolt fighter. Weighing anything up to 17,500 lb loaded, the P-47 usually achieved 425 mph at around 30,000 ft, had plummeting acceleration in the dive, a lightning roll which offset to some extent the moderate turning circle, and a reputation for absorbing fantastic punishment and still getting home. Thunderbolts played a big part in the European Theatre of Operations during 1943/44 in scything away the German fighter screens which previously had been crippling the U.S. 8th Air Force heavy-bomber daylight offensive over Germany. So much so that in the spring of 1944, U.S. aces like Major Robert S. Johnson of the 56th Fighter Group experienced frustrating periods when mission after mission was flown with only token aerial opposition from the *Luftwaffe*.

Johnson was a born 'ace', with an aggressive spirit tempered in the boxing ring and on the football field, a marksman's eye, and keen vision which often enabled him to spot an enemy formation before himself being seen. He was a fine

A P-47D Thunderbolt takes off, showing its massive, wide-track main undercarriage. The size of the pilot emphasises the giant proportions of the machine.

flier, a leader whose proud claim was that he never lost a wingman. Yet he actually had signed on for bombers after joining the AAF in November 1941, and his assignment to the very first Thunderbolt unit, the 56th Fighter Group, came as a welcome surprise. With the 61st Squadron of the 56th, he went to England in January 1943.

Royal Air Force pilots, and even Spitfire-flying American Eagle Squadron fliers, were incredulous at and dubious about the sheer bulk of the P-47. Fighter Command was often having a bad time at the hands of picked German units flying the deadly Focke-Wulf Fw 190. Too few of the new Spitfire IXs were available, and the main British fighter was still the 375-mph Spitfire V, outdistanced, out-gunned, and outrolled by the 190. Spitfire pilots dismally forecast that the P-47, with its sluggish climb and moderate turning circle, would be easy meat for a good Focke-Wulf pilot. And while the P-47s were learning the deadly business of air combat they did take some losses. But this position was dramatically reversed when the American pilots gained battle experience, and high-flying Thunderbolts built up an astonishing proportion of

kills to losses over the next year or so. The 56th—Hub Zemke's Wolf-pack—finally gave first place only to the 4th Fighter Group (incorporating the original Eagle squadrons) in the 8th Air Force's fifteen fighter groups in terms of enemy aircraft destroyed.

After a slow start dogged by poor luck, Johnson attained a score of 28 kills, most of them single-seater fighters, in just about a year on operations with the 56th, becoming the second highest individual U.S. scorer in the E.T.O., and in record time. He had his full share of narrow escapes and used up five Thunderbolts during his tour with the 56th. One machine was labelled 'All Hell', another 'Lucky', and one of the latest machines he used was 'Penrod and Sam', a P-47-21-RE serialled 42-25512, illustrated here. Overall finish of this plane was natural metal, with the usual blue and white star and bar insignia, and dark green anti-dazzle panel on the decking forward of the cockpit. The nose bore the 56th's red identi-fication band and the rubber was yellow. The code letters LM-Q and the fin serial number were black, as was the nickname 'Penrod and Sam'

A P-47D of a training unit in the U.S.A. in 1943.

Later production models in the P-47D range featured a cut down rear fuselage and a teardrop cockpit canopy which gave 360-degree vision about the upper hemisphere.

Another late D model P-47 showing fuselage and wing-mounted droppable long range fuel tanks.

(picked out with white relief on the red band) carried on the port nose cowling only. Twenty-five red victory symbols, German crosses, were carried at this particular time on the fuselage side below the cockpit. This was probably the machine Johnson flew on his last mission with the 56th, on 8 May 1944, when he downed his last two enemy fighters. A delayed confirmation came through later which, with these two, totalled 28 kills.

The Thunderbolt D series, from 1 to 22, were produced in greater numbers than any other; 3963 were made. A P-47D-1-RE squadron machine tested in England achieved 406 mph at 27,000 ft. and climbed at 1650 ft per min at sea level, dropping to 840 ft per min at 28,700 ft. Climb to 30,000 ft took 22.9 min and the estimated ceiling was 36,100 ft, all this with the turbo-supercharged 2000-hp R-2800-21 Double Wasp radial. Water injection on its R-2800-59 engine (2300 hp war emergency wet at 27,000 ft) and a 'paddle'-blade airscrew gave the 21-RE a much better performance, as the following specifications show.

P-47D-21-RE: span 40 ft $9\frac{5}{16}$ in; length 36 ft 1¾ in; height 14 ft 2 in; wing area 300 sq ft; maximum speeds (with water injection, brief period only) 433 mph at 30,000 ft, 421 mph at 25,000 ft; 390 mph at 15,000 ft; 353 mph at 5000 ft; rate of climb on water injection 2750 ft per min at 5000 ft reducing to 1375 ft per min at 30,000 ft; landing speed 92-106 mph according to load; maximum tankage 680 gallons (internal 305 gallon plus two 150-gallon wing drop tanks and 75-gallon belly tank); bomb load (alternative to drop tanks) up to three 500-lb bombs; armament six or eight .5-in machine guns, 267 (normal) or 425 (maximum) rounds per gun; maximum range 1725 miles at 10,000 ft at 16,200 lb take-off weight (680 gallon) at maximum economy cruise power reducing to 900 miles at maximum continuous power. Range with bombs but with no extra tanks was approximately halved.

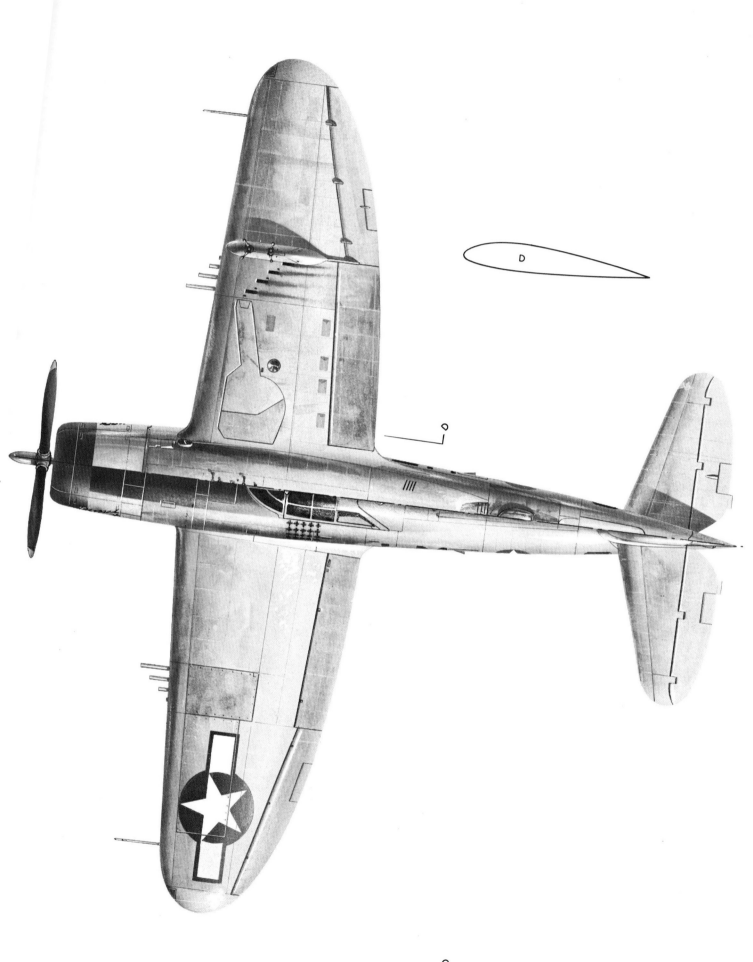

D

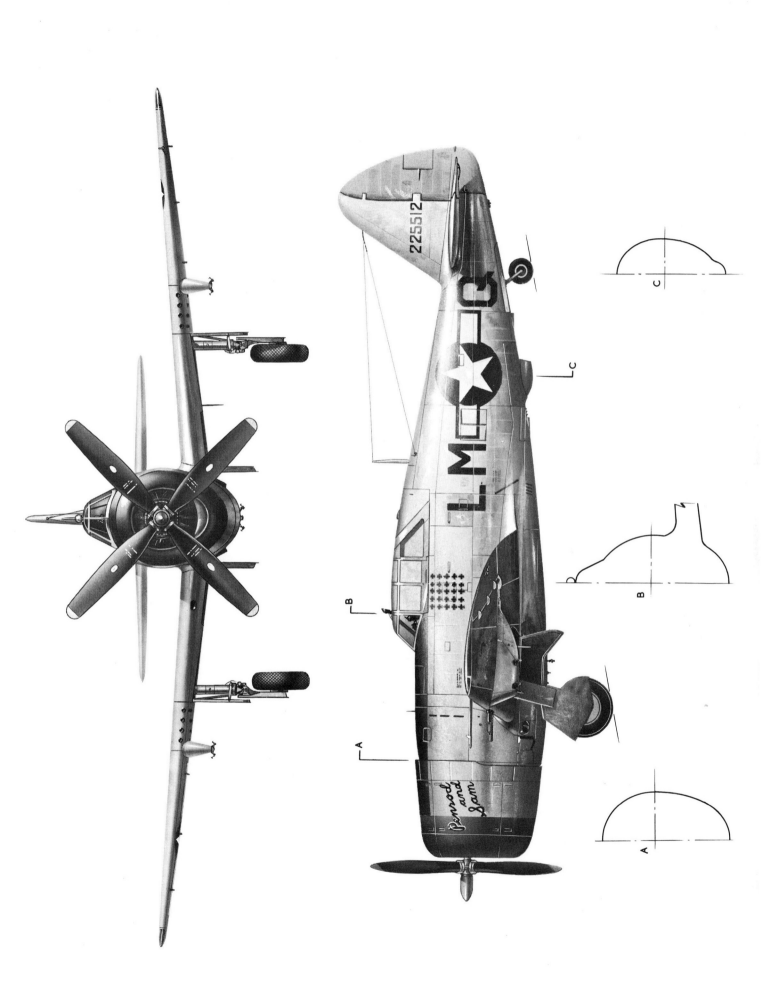

Past the Sound Barrier Charles Yeager and the Bell X-1

Captain Charles E. Yeager stands behind the Bell X-1A.

IN THE YEARS JUST PRIOR to the Second World War, test pilots and aeronautical engineers began to encounter a new obstacle in their quest for ever increasing speeds. In power dives and other sudden accelerations, planes became uncontrollable, were buffeted and sometimes broken by the newly encountered phenomenon of compressibility.

The interrelation of compressibility shock waves with Mach numbers was theoretically understood, but practical means of overcoming completely what a British aerodynamicist dubbed the 'sound barrier' were still a decade away.

Then came the war, and high-speed projects were started by several of the major combatants as the piercing of this barrier to safe higher speeds became a vital military necessity. The new jet and rocket power sources under development made the problem still more urgent.

Brilliant work in Germany evolved the swept-wing concept, which though only a palliative promised to give the Germans a commanding lead in the design of high-speed military aircraft. In England, Miles Aircraft Ltd. designed—to a 1943 Air Ministry specification—a 1000-mph research aeroplane with such revolutionary features as a bi-convex wing section, 'slab' tailplane, power-boosted controls, automatically-recorded test instrumentation, a pressurised capsule cockpit, and a gigantic ducted-fan afterburning jet engine of 17,000 ebhp. Had the war continued, there would have developed a neck-and-neck race between Germany, Britain and the U.S.A to get the first aircraft through the sound barrier. Defeat halted the German progress, and the British project was shelved when nearly completed in 1946 in favour of a timid and abortive programme with airborne models which put England years behind in the supersonic race.

Soviet Russia despoiled German aircraft plants in 1945 and claimed in May 1947 that one of her aircraft had exceeded the speed of sound—whether in a dive or level flight was never made clear.

In the United States, the NACA had suggested as early as 1943 that a research airplane be built to explore the transonic region. Robert A. Wolf of Bell Aircraft Corporation attended the NACA conference of 18 December 1943, and later emphasised his views on the need for such a

The Bell X-1 gliding to earth above the Muroc test base.

high-speed project in a letter to Dr George W. Lewis, then NACA director of aeronautical research. By April 1944, Bell had a proposal on paper which was sent to NACA.

Supersonic speed capabilities for the design were broached later by Robert J. Woods, Bell's chief design engineer, at a meeting with Major Ezra Kotcher, a project officer at Wright Field. Kotcher revealed that a 6000 lb st turbo-rocket was under development by one of the engine companies which would provide the needed power, and Woods returned to his firm to persuade Larry Bell to start the 800-mph MX-524 project, later amended to MX-653.

This design finally evolved as a simple man-carrying rocket-powered aircraft—the turbo-rocket would not have been ready in time—with straight wings and an orthodox structure, but with quite extraordinary strength factors of around 18g positive and 10g negative. Air launching and skid landing gear were considered, but possible military applications, if the design were successful, dictated a conventional tricycle landing gear. It was thought that wing wake interference over the tail would present one of the biggest problems of transonic flight, and therefore the tail was placed fairly high on the fin and made readily adjustable to counter-act trim changes.

The power unit was a Reaction Motors RMI-6000C4 rocket engine having four tubes each of 1500 lb st operating at a chamber pressure of about 230 lb/sq in. The unit could not be throttled and so power was varied by burning one, two, three or all four tubes.

Choice of propellants fell on liquid oxygen and alcohol; both were easily obtainable, had good power potential, were not spontaneously combustible and were relatively safe to handle by

Above and below:
The second X-1 was used by N.A.C.A. for high speed flight research and was later rebuilt as X-1E.

ground-crews. Design of a complicated turbine-driven pump threatened to delay the programme, so initially a system of pressurising the propellant tanks from an array of compressed nitrogen bottles was employed. Appropriately regulated, the nitrogen also raised and lowered the undercarriage and flaps, drove the gyros for the flight instruments, actuated the tailplane screw jack and topped up cabin pressure. The nitrogen system put up the weight by 2000 lb and reduced endurance by over 1½ minutes but prevented delay in the start of first flight tests.

To preserve the bullet shape of the forward fuselage, the cockpit canopy was actually part of

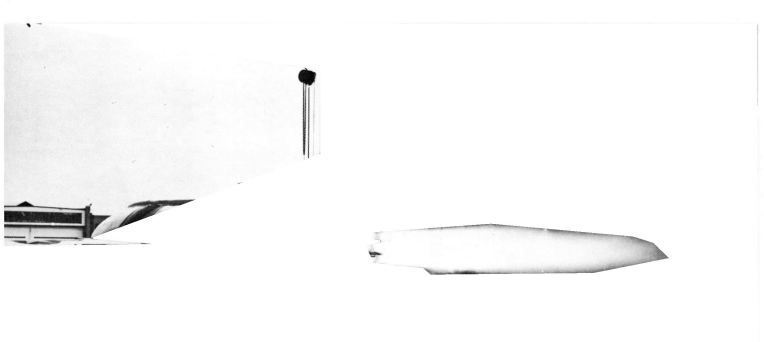

Ground firing tests of the rocket motor installed in the Bell X-1.

the fuselage decking. Plexiglas, used to avoid difficulties in producing double-curvature plate glass, later encountered trouble with aerodynamic heating, and in the X-1A redesign a conventional canopy with plate glass screen was substituted.

The cockpit was pressurised only to about 3 lb/sq in above atmosphere to minimise injury to the pilot if the cockpit were punctured.

The end of the war made available a B-29 for the air launching that Bell engineers had originally envisaged. The B-29 could take the plane up to operating altitude, conserving the rocket fuel supply and avoiding the dangers of a take-off at a 100-lb/sq ft wing loading. Bomb doors and part of the belly of the B-29 were cut away and the X-1 suspended beneath from a standard bomb shackle.

Air tests had to be made first to see whether the X-1 would separate cleanly from the mother ship. Pressure surveys using the X-1's port wing pressure orifices were carried out and it seemed that a positive separating force did exist, but to make sure, guide and ejection gear was evolved to aid separation.

In February 1946 the first drop and glide tests were made by Jack Woolams. Muroc Dry Lake was flooded at this time of year, and so Pinecastle, Fla., was the site chosen. The engineless X-1 was launched on its first flight at about 27,000 ft, glided to the ground in twelve minutes and landed at about 110 mph. Ten glide flights were made at Pinecastle, followed by four more at Muroc, where test facilities meantime had been prepared. Then, on 9 December 1946, in perfect weather, the X-1 was launched at 27,000 ft for its first powered flight, when it reached Mach 0.79 piloted by Chalmers S. Goodlin. Bell pilots

Goodlin and 'Tex' Johnson took the plane to over Mach 0.8 and pulled 8g before finally handing over the first plane (6602) to the air force. The second model, 6603, was eventually given to NACA for supplementary research and piloted in the main by Herbert H. Hoover and Howard C. Lilley. The third model, 6604, was waiting for the turbine-driven pump, but on its first flight later was jettisoned from the B-29 and blew up after a mid-air fire.

Responsibility for the air force testing of the X-1 was given to the Fighter Test Section at the Flight Test Laboratory, Wright-Patterson AFB. Careful combing of the group of pilots attached to the Section finally isolated an unassuming young officer noted for his emotional stability and precision flying, Captain Charles E. Yeager.

Born on 13 February 1923 at Myra, West Virginia, Yeager joined the air force in September 1941. He had had no special ambition to fly, but the idea being implanted by a friend and encouraged by his father, it soon became the thing he most wanted to do. Commissioned as Flight Officer in March 1943, he went to England with the 363rd Fighter Squadron in November 1943. On his eighth mission, 4 March 1944, he shot down his first Bf 109 and damaged an He 111. On his ninth mission the next day, he had to jump by parachute from his burning plane over southern France, evading capture and being helped towards the Spanish border by French partisans. He won the Bronze Star for helping a wounded comrade across the border, and finally arrived back in England just

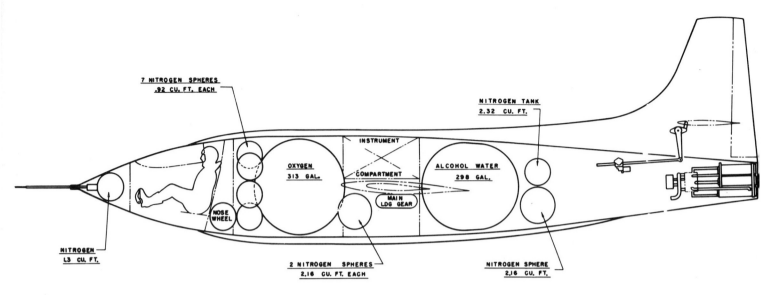

Labels on diagram:
7 NITROGEN SPHERES .92 CU. FT. EACH
NITROGEN TANK 2.32 CU. FT.
INSTRUMENT
OXYGEN 313 GAL.
COMPARTMENT
ALCOHOL WATER 298 GAL.
NOSE WHEEL
MAIN LDG GEAR
NITROGEN L3 CU. FT.
2 NITROGEN SPHERES 2.16 CU. FT. EACH
NITROGEN SPHERE 2.16 CU. FT.

A diagrammatic view of the Bell X-1 showing the disposition of equipment and fuel tanks.

before D-Day. Getting permission direct from Washington, against all the rules, to rejoin his old unit, Yeager eventually won the Silver Star and Cluster, Distinguished Flying Cross with two clusters, the Purple Heart, and other decorations, in all flew 64 combat missions in Mustangs totalling 270 combat hours, and downed a further 11 enemy aircraft. March 1945 saw him returning to the States, to take a pilot instructor's course at Perrin Field, Texas, followed by a two-month period as basic flying instructor there, and then a transfer to the Fighter Test Section.

Yeager made his first X-1 flight in August 1947. The plane was empty of fuel and Lox, the flight being to familiarize him with the plane's handling

The four-chamber Reaction Motors RMI-6000C4 rocket engine.

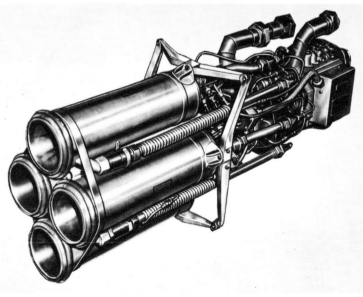

qualities and the deadstick landing pattern with its 200-220 mph approach speed. Following two further preliminary glide flights, the machine was fuelled, and Yeager dropped out and began to feel out the motor. On three chambers he climbed to 40,000 ft and rapidly attained Mach 0.867 before shutting down. His test programme called for a controlled inching forward, each step being checked and doubled-checked with the recorded instrument data and his air force, NACA and Bell team-mates. A camera was mounted over his shoulder to photograph the instrument panel. Instruments in the amidships bay recorded pressure over the surfaces as well as aileron and elevator positions and forces, and a telemetering device transmitted all this data back to the ground.

On the second flight, to Mach 0.89, buffeting was encountered and also a wing drop which needed one-third aileron to correct. On the third flight 0.91 was recorded. On the fourth, at 0.94 the plane could not be turned from its straight path. In the vertical bank ready for the turn, the elevators were powerless at that speed due to shock waves forming over them. So Yeager tried moving the whole horizontal stabiliser on the next flight, and used the same successful technique, too, to cure pitch-up. Conventional elevators were thus proved virtually useless in the transonic region and so a slab or flying tail came to be used on modern transonic and supersonic aircraft.

On the sixth flight, 14 October 1947, Yeager 'kicked it up to about Mach 1.04'—his own laconic words to describe one of the most epoch-making flights since the first powered one of all by the Wrights in 1903.

The ride through to Mach 1.0 was pretty rough at times, and Yeager had some nasty moments during some of the 80 or so flights made on the X-1. The maximum speed reached by the original

machines was Mach 1.5, 976 mph at 46,000 ft, and the best height attained was 70,000 ft, both figures well above those originally envisaged for the project.

Yeager's last X-1 flight on 5 January 1949 was risky as well as spectacular, a ground take-off, judged by Bell engineers to be so dangerous because of the machine's high wing loading and the chance of a power cut near the ground. Averaging a

The X-1 in flight with motor burning.

The Bell X-1A nestles beneath the belly of the giant Boeing mother plane. Charles Yeager flew this machine to Mach 2.51 (1650 mph) on 12 December 1953.

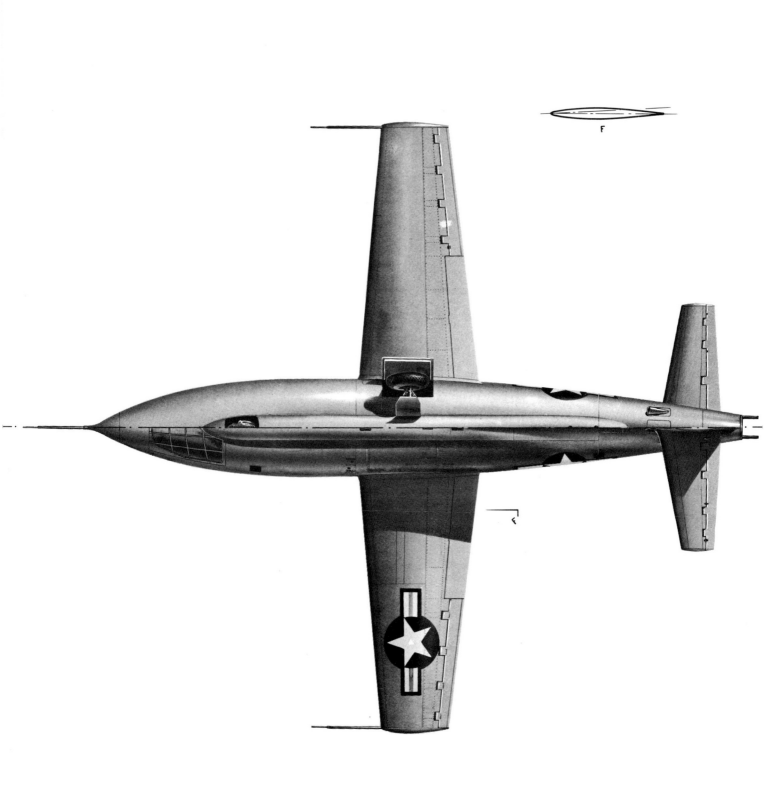

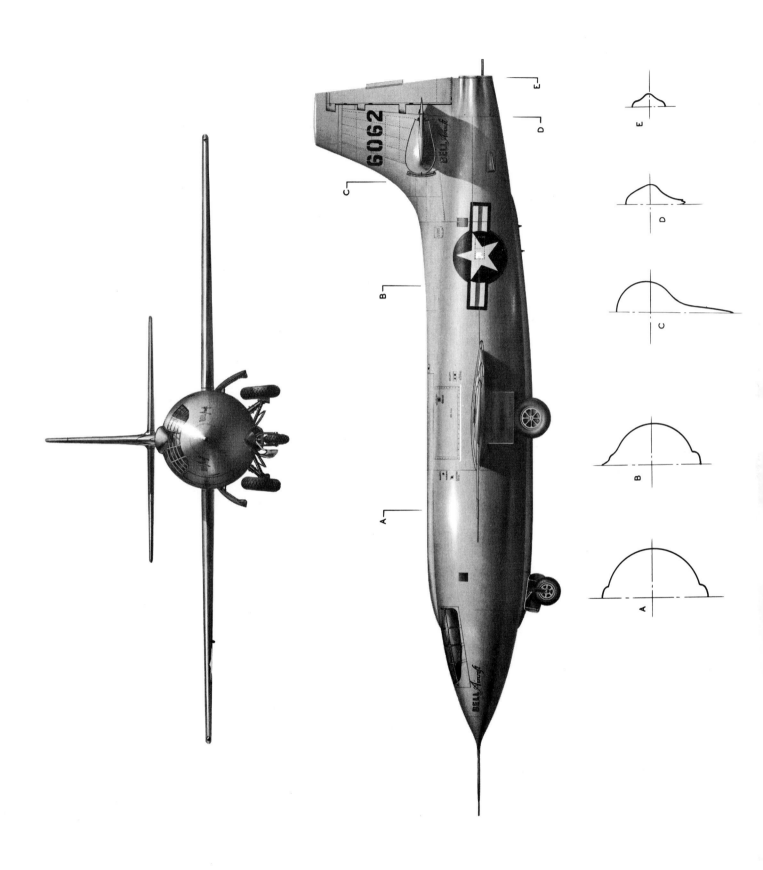

Redesign of the X-1 resulted in the X-1A and B versions.
The X-1B was five feet longer than the original machine.
had a redesigned nose and cockpit area, more fuel and a
turbine pump to force-feed propellants to the rocket motor.
It was flown to Mach 2.3 in 1954 by Frank Everest.

climb rate exceeding 13,000 ft per min, the X-1 reached 23,000 ft in 1 min 40 sec before the half-load of propellant gave out.

'Chuck' Yeager later flew the revised X-1A on four flights, and on the last 'over-stepped his bounds a bit' and reached Mach 2.51, about 1650 mph, on 12 December 1953. He had already received the 1949 Collier's Trophy—with Lawrence D. Bell and NACA's John Stack—for his part in the X-1 project, and the Mackay Trophy for his first supersonic flight. Now he was awarded the Harmon Trophy by the President of the United States and also the Distinguished Service Medal in recognition of his contributions to science.

The time now came for him to resume his normal air force career, and on 3 October 1954 he was assigned to the 12th Air Force HQ in Germany.

The X-1 was finally installed in the National Air Museum, Smithsonian Institution, along with the Wright Biplane and the *Spirit of St Louis,* and 'Chuck' Yeager has the same assured place, with the Wrights and Charles Lindbergh, as one of the greatest aviators of this aeronautical age. Dimensions of the original X-1s were: span 28 ft; length 30 ft 10.98 in; height 10 ft 10.2 in. Wing area was 130 sq ft and wing thickness 8% on 6602 and 10% on 6603. Varying figures were given for weights, etc., as modifications were made during the lengthy development and trial period. The following are believed to be approximate for the machine at the time of the great 14 October flight: empty weight 6890 lb including 526 lb of test equipment; loaded weight 13,400 lb; wing loadings, 103 lb/sq ft take-off, and 55 lb/sq ft landing; full power endurance, 2.5 minutes; landing speed usually around 180 mph; flaps up stalling speed 240 mph. The plane was coloured a bright orange.